Bloom's Literary Guide

DUBLIN
LONDON
NEW YORK
PARIS
ROME

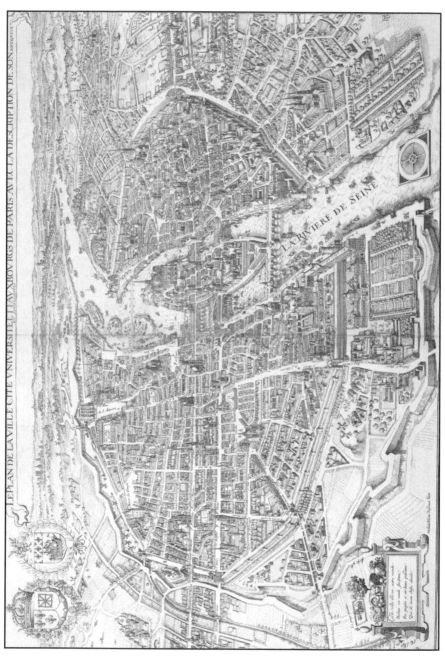

Plan de Merian–1615. Though popular, this map by Merian provides more of an overview of Paris rather than an accurate representation of the city.

Bloom's Literary Guide to

PARIS

Mike Gerrard

Introduction by
Harold Bloom

Checkmark Books
An imprint of Infobase Publishing

Bloom's Literary Guide to Paris

Checkmark Books
An imprint of Infobase Publishing
132 West 31st Street
New York NY 10001

Library of Congress Cataloging-in-Publication Data

Gerrard, Mike.
  Paris / Mike Gerrard; edited by Harold Bloom.
    p. cm. — (Bloom's literary guide)
  ISBN 0-7910-9379-4 (pbk.)
    1. Paris (France)—In literature. 2. Paris (France)—Civilization.
  3. French literature—History and criticism. I. Bloom, Harold.
  II. Title. III. Series.
  DC715.G435 2007
  944'.631—dc22   2007017699

Series and cover design by Takeshi Takahashi

Printed in the United States of America

Bang EJB 10 9 8 7 6 5 4 3 2 1

This book is printed on acid-free paper.

TABLE OF CONTENTS

HAROLD **BLOOM**

Cities of the Mind

It could be argued that the ancestral city for the Western literary imagination is neither Athens nor Jerusalem, but ancient Alexandria, where Hellenism and Hebraism fused and were harvested. All Western writers of authentic aesthetic eminence are Alexandrians, whether they know it or not. Proust and Joyce, Flaubert and Goethe, Shakespeare and Dante rather uneasily share in that eclectic heritage. From the mid third century before the Common Era through the mid third century after, Alexandria was the city of the spirit and mind, where Plato and Moses did not reconcile (which would be impossible) but abrasively stimulated a new kind of sensibility, that we have learned to call Modernism, now twenty-six centuries old. The first Modernist was the poet Callimachus, who said that a long poem was a long evil, and together with his colleagues were approvingly named as *neoteroi* (modernists) by Aristarchus, the earliest literary critic to attempt making a secular canon. Dr. Samuel Johnson, Boileau, Sainte-Beuve, Lessing, Coleridge, I.A. Richards, Empson, Kenneth Burke are descendants of Aristarchus.

F.E. Peters, in his lucid *The Harvest of Hellenism*, summarizes the achievement of Hellenistic Alexandria by an impressive catalog: "Gnosticism, the university, the catechetical school, pastoral poetry, monasticism, the romance, grammar, lexicography, city planning, theology, canon law, heresy and scholasticism". I don't know why Peters omitted neo-Platonism, inaugurated by Plotinius, and I myself already have added literary criticism, and further would list the library. Alexandria has now exiled its Greeks, Jews, and mostly everyone else not an Arab, and so it is no longer the city of the mind, and of the poetic tradition that went the long span from Callimachus to Cavafy. Yet we cannot arrive at a true appreciation of literary places unless we begin with Alexandria. I recommend the novelist E.M. Forster's guide to the city, which deeply ponders its cultural significance.

We are all Alexandrians, as even Dante was, since he depended upon Hellenistic Neo-Platonic interpretations of Homer, whose poetry he had never read. Vergil, Dante's guide, was Hellenistic in culture, and followed Theocritus in pastoral, and Alexandrian imitations of Homer in epic. But though our literary culture remains Alexandrian (consider all our ongoing myths of Modernism), we follow St. Augustine in seeing Jerusalem as the City of God, of King David and his martyred descendant Jesus of Nazareth. Our universities, inescapably Alexandrian in their pragmatic eclecticism, nevertheless continue to exalt the Athens of Socrates, Plato, and Aristotle as the city of cognition and of (supposed) democracy. The actual Periclean Athens was a slave-owning oligarchy and plutocracy, which still prevails in much of the world, be it Saudia Arabia or many of the Americas. Literary Athens, in its Golden Age, built on Homer and produced the only Western drama that can challenge Shakespeare: Aeschylus, Euripides, Sophocles and the divine Aristophanes (I follow Heinrich Heine who observed that: "There is a God and his name is Aristophanes".)

Athens now slumbers except for Olympic games and tourism, while Jerusalem is all too lively as the center of Israeli-Arab contention. Alas, their literary glories have waned, but so have those of Rome, where Vergil and even the Florentine Dante are little read or emulated. Cities of the mind are still represented by Paris and London, both perhaps at this moment in cognitive decline. The international language is now American English, and New York City is therefore the literary place-of-places. That, of necessity, has mixed consequences, but those sharpen my renewed comparison to ancient Alexandria, which mingled inventiveness with high decadence, at the end of an age. Alexandria was consciously belated and so are we, despite our paradoxical ecstasy of the new.

2

Is a literary place, by pragmatic definition, a city? Pastoral, like all other literary forms, was an urban invention. The Hebrew Bible, redacted in Babylonian exile, has as its core in Genesis, Exodus, Numbers, the Yahwist's narrative composed at Solomon's highly sophisticated court in Jerusalem. We cannot locate the inception of what became *Iliad* and *Odyssey*, but the Greece they taught centered at Athens and Thebes. Florence exiled Dante and Cavalcanti, yet shared all further vernacular literary development with Rome and Milan. If Montaigne tended to isolate himself from embattled Paris, he knew his readers remained there. Elizabethan-Jacobean literature is virtually all fixated upon London, and centers upon Shakespeare's Globe Theater. If the American Renaissance emanates out of the Concord of Emerson, Thoreau, Hawthorne, it is equally at home in the New York City of Whitman, Melville, and the burgeoning James family. Though Faulkner kept, as much as he could, to Oxford, Mississippi, and Wallace Stevens to Hartford, if I had to nominate the ultimate classic of the United States in the twentieth century, unhesitatingly I would choose the poetry of Hart Crane, Whitman's legitimate heir as the bard of New York City. Kenneth Burke, whenever I saw him from 1975 on, would assure me again that Whitman's "Crossing Brooklyn Ferry" and Hart Crane's *The Bridge* were the two greatest American poems.

Our best living novelists—Philip Roth, Pynchon, DeLillo—have become inseparable from the ethos of New York City. Only the elusive Cormac McCarthy, seer of *Blood Meridian*, keeps far away from the city-of-cities, which has displaced London and Paris as the world's imaginative capital.

3

However solitary a major writer is by vocation, he or she tends to find a closest friend in a contemporary literary artist. Perhaps rivals attract: Shakespeare and Ben Jonson, Byron and Shelley, Hawthorne and Melville, Hemingway and Scott Fitzgerald, Eliot and Pound, Hart Crane and Allen Tate are just a few pairings, to stay within Anglo-American tradition. Yet the tendency is everywhere: Goethe and Schiller, Wordsworth and Coleridge, Swift and Pope, Tolstoy and Chekhov, Henry James and Edith Wharton, and many more, too numerous to list. The locales waver: Hemingway and Fitzgerald in Paris, Byron and Shelley in Italian exile together, Eliot and Pound in London. There are giant exceptions: Cervantes, Milton, Victor Hugo, Emily Dickinson, Joyce and Beckett (though only after their early association).

Cities are the essential requisite for literary relationships, including those dominated by a father-figure, the London assemblage of the Sons of Ben Jonson: Carew, Lovelace, Herrick, Suckling, Randoph and many more, or Dr. Samuel Johnson and his club of Boswell, Goldsmith, Burke, among others, or Mallarmé and his disciples, including Valéry, who was to surpass his master. Modernist London always calls up Bloomsbury, with Virginia Woolf as its luminous figure, the ornament of a group that in its own idiosyncratic mode saw E.M. Forster as its patriarch.

Even in the age of the computer screen, proximity is essential for literary fellowship. But so far I have considered the city as literary place only in regard to writers. As subject, indeed as *the given* of literature, the city is a larger matter. The movement from garden to city as literary focus is powerfully clear in the

Hebrew Bible, when Yahweh moves his abode from Mount Sinai to Mount Zion, and thus to Solomon's Temple. As the mountain of the Covenant, Sinai stands at the origin, but surprisingly Ezekiel (28:13 following) locates "Eden, the garden of God" as a plateau on Zion, both cosmological mountain and paradise. When Yahweh takes up residence in the Temple, his Eden is close by, yet nevertheless the transition from garden to city has been accomplished. This is the Holy City, but to the literary imagination all the great cities are sacred: Paris, London, Dublin, Petersburg, Rome, and New York are also sanctified, whatever suffering and inequity transpire in them.

4

In the United States the national capital, Washington D.C., is scarcely a city of the mind, not only when contrasted to New York City, but also to Boston, Chicago, San Francisco. Paris, London, Rome are at once capitals and literary centers, but Washington D.C. has harbored few major American writers and has provided subjects only for political novelists, like Henry Adams and Gore Vidal. The Great American Novel perpetually remains to be written, despite such earlier splendors as *The Scarlet Letter, Moby-Dick, Huckleberry Finn*, and *The Portrait of a Lady*, and a handful of later masterpieces from *As I Lay Dying* and *The Sound and the Fury, The Sun Also Rises* and *The Great Gatsby*, on to *Gravity's Rainbow, Sabbath's Theater, Underworld*, and *Blood Meridian*. I rather doubt that it will take Washington, D.C. as subject, or be composed by an inhabitant thereof.

The industrialization of the great cities in the nineteenth century gave us the novels of Victor Hugo, Dickens, Zola which produced a realism totally phantasmagoric, now probably no longer available to us. Computer urbanism does not seem likely to stimulate imaginative literature. Visual overdetermination overwhelms the inward eye and abandons us to narrative or the formal splendors of poetry and drama. There is something hauntingly elegiac about fresh evocations of literary places, here and now in the early years of the Twenty-first century.

HAROLD **BLOOM**

Introduction

When I think of Paris as a literary context, the first writers who suggest themselves to me are Balzac, Victor Hugo, Baudelaire, and Zola. So much of the strongest French literature is Parisian that second thoughts make me wonder at not turning to Villon, Molière, Cornielle, Racine, Voltaire, Diderot, Stendhal, Flaubert, Mallarmé, Rimbaud, Proust, Valéry. Literary Paris is inconceivable without that dozen, but if one broods on Paris at its imaginative best, the fourfold of Balzac, Hugo, Baudelaire, Zola seems unassailable. The grand thematic of Parisian literature is social alienation, or the psychic distance between the imagination and society. That seems to me less true of Shakespeare's London and Walt Whitman's New York City, though one should observe that no French imaginative writer is as central a figure in Parisian sensibility as Shakespeare and Whitman are to their cities. Descartes occupies the mind of France and is emblematic of Parisian consciousness as profoundly as Shakespeare is England and Walt Whitman is America. Even Victor Hugo, Balzac, and Baudelaire together are not the giant forms of Shakespeare and of Whitman.

To choose a single French writer who would be as universal a figure, able to compete with Dante and Shakespeare, Tolstoy and Cervantes, Goethe and Whitman, Ibsen and Joyce, you would need to fuse Montaigne (who tried to avoid Paris) and Molière. And yet Balzac, Hugo, Baudelaire, and Zola can be combined into a fourfold image, akin to Blake's Four Zoas or the cherubim of Ezekiel's chariot. Nineteenth-century Paris, viewed through the novels of Balzac, Hugo, Zola and the poems of Hugo and Baudelaire, becomes a phantasmagoric vision, frighteningly pulsating with vitality as with a societal entropy and degradation. Balzac and Hugo in particular recall the giants of Rabelais, breaking out of all restraint in quest of utopian and humanistic fulfillment.

Balzac found in Paris the kingdom of this world, and exulted in revealing it. "He hides nothing", Proust marvels, "he says everything". Whether even Paris, in his day, had as much energy of spirit as the preternatural Balzac did, can reasonably be doubted. There are ninety novels, large and small, in *The Human Comedy*, and they might have been two hundred had not overwork killed Balzac at fifty. His Paris was his own exuberant creation, rather as though Milton's Satan and Shakespeare's Falstaff had combined their personal energies into a social reality.

Victor Hugo, like Balzac, can seem less an actual person than a Shakespearean character. Certainly his heroic stance and presence during the Paris Commune of 1871 can be seen now as representative of him as Walt Whitman's emblem was his Civil War volunteer service in the hospitals of Washington D.C. Hugo's High Romanticism made him the poet-novelist of the Communard barricades, and fulfilled the vision worked out in *Les Misérables* (1862). So vast in scope is Hugo's total range of writing that no single reader can encompass it. I love Hugo's poetry, but there are rather more than one hundred and fifty five thousand lines of it, as well as seven novels, at least twenty plays, and a mountain of discursive prose. There is no wonder that Charles Baudelaire suffered from a sense of being crowded out by Victor Hugo, who took up all of literary space by and for himself.

And yet Hugo is so cosmological that he transcends Paris, so that Baudelaire becomes as much the poet of Paris as Balzac is its novelist. Hugo, an exile from Napoleon III, was termed by Baudelaire "a genius without frontiers", but the apolitical poet of *Les fleurs du mal* (1857, 1861) was an alienated internal exile. His Paris can seem *the* Paris, as Whitman's seems *the* Manhattan. Isolated, walking the streets of an infernal city, Baudelaire creates the aesthetic ethos of modern Paris. Hugo, from his exile on the Channel Island of Jersey, prophesied in the modes of Isaiah and Jeremiah, in the expectation of being vindicated by history. Composing the poems of his moment, while denying progress, protest and history, Baudelaire anticipated the literary future as Hugo could not.

I end with Emile Zola in 1877, when he brought out *L' assommoir*, which provoked furious outrage by its new perspectives upon working-class life. Bourgeois fury at the loss of the novel to the unwashed scarcely could have been more vociferous. The spirit of the Paris Commune revived in Zola's work, even more powerfully in *Germinal* (1885). Something implied in Balzac, and pushed aside by Baudelaire's subjectivity, culminates in Zola's visionary Realism.

New Haven, CT   HAROLD BLOOM
July 2004

CHAPTER | **ONE**

Paris Today

Whether it's April in Paris or Paris in the fall, the French capital has inspired writers at all times of year throughout its history. It is known as one of the most beautiful and romantic cities in the world, dubbed the City of Light, and perhaps only Venice can rival its effect on visitors. No one can fail to be enchanted by that first sight of the Eiffel Tower. Paris's many long-renowned structures, such as the Louvre and the Arc de Triomphe, contrast in a variety of ways with the city's more modern sights, such as the Pompidou Center, putting the rich history of the city into dramatic relief: this new arts center literally turned architectural convention inside-out and created quite a stir when it was first built in 1977, with its normal interior features—including escalators and air ducts—all colorfully visible on the outside. Perhaps the strength of the city's traditions in all the arts provide its painters and poets, its fashion designers and filmmakers, with the incentive and the authority required to take the kind of risk the Pompidou exemplifies.

The Pompidou Center is just one example of Parisian innovativeness, and in fact, Paris gave us the expression *avant-garde* to describe anything that is forward thinking. At the same time, however, Parisians remain true to their traditions, preserving even in their everyday conversation certain niceties of social decorum. For example, it is considered rude not to greet someone with *bonjour* (good day) or *bonsoir* (good evening) before starting a conversation. And the most eccentric productions of Paris's avant-garde are often in a sense the most radically respectful of the traditions from which they depart.

Paris also has a long tradition in tourism, and the city is full of attractions; its many art galleries and museums are especially famous. Paris is an easy city to get around in, with an inexpensive *métro* (subway) system that goes almost everywhere. Often people prefer to walk, however, because the city is compact and it offers so many beautiful sights, especially by the banks of the River Seine, which runs right through the center of Paris.

ARRONDISSEMENTS AND MUSEUMS

Paris was first divided into districts, known as *arrondissements*, in 1790. At that time there were 48 *arrondissements*, but today there are just 20. They are numbered consecutively and radiate out from the city's center.

The 1st district is roughly in the geographical center of the city. In the pre-revolutionary days when France was a monarchy, this district was where the French royal families lived. The Palais-Royal (Royal Palace) was the childhood home of King Louis XIV and later of King Louis-Philippe. Today it houses government offices, although the courtyard can still be visited. Close by is the Louvre, which was also originally a royal palace; today it is famous for having one of the world's greatest art collections.

Almost opposite the Louvre, on the other side of the river, is Paris's other great art gallery: the Musée d'Orsay. This stylish space was once a railway station and has been brilliantly converted into a museum to complement the Louvre. Covering a more modern period of the arts from 1848 to 1914, the Musée d'Orsay holds one of the world's best collections of impressionist artwork.

More modern still in its collections is the Pompidou Center, roughly half a mile due east of the Louvre. The Pompidou Center houses the National Museum of Modern Art, but it also has a movie theater, a program of temporary exhibitions, and an excellent art bookshop. The open space outside the museum attracts street performers and crowds alike.

POPULAR DISTRICTS

One of the most popular districts for visitors these days is the Marais, about one mile southeast of the Louvre along one of the city's most famous streets, the rue de Rivoli. The Marais is one of the city's oldest quarters and contains perhaps the city's loveliest square, the place des Vosges. There are also numerous museums, including the Victor Hugo Museum in the author's former home, right on the place des Vosges.

Almost two miles (3 km) due north of the Louvre is another district that most visitors usually, and understandably, want to see: Montmartre. This slightly elevated area, a kind of village almost, has long been the home of the city's artists. The painters Henri Toulouse-Lautrec, Vincent van Gogh, Edgar Dégas, and Maurice Utrillo have all called this district home. Many of them frequented the clubs and cabarets that also flourished there, including the infamous Moulin Rouge, which still exists today. Also in Montmartre is the church of Sacré-Coeur, another notable Paris landmark. From the front of the church is a splendid view across the city, making it a popular spot on weekends.

The magnificent Notre-Dame Cathedral is the other great church that tourists typically flock to see. Construction on it was begun in 1163 and completed in 1330. When it later fell into disrepair, Victor Hugo was instrumental in raising funds and campaigning to have it restored. He also wrote a book about the cathedral, whose French title, *Notre-Dame de Paris*, is lesser known than the English translation, *The Hunchback of Notre-Dame*.

Notre-Dame dominates the Île de la Cité, one of two small islands that stand in the River Seine. The smaller Île St-Louis is full of atmospheric backstreets, while the Île de la Cité contains not only the Notre-Dame Cathedral, but also the church of Sainte-Chapelle. It has one of the world's finest collections of stained glass, the Conciergerie. This church was also used as a prison at the time of the French Revolution and as the headquarters of the city's police force. Close by is the Police Judiciaire, the Paris detective force where Georges Simenon's famous fictional detective, Inspector Maigret, was based.

THE LANDMARKS OF PARIS

About two miles (3 km) due west of the Île de la Cité, past the golden dome of the Dôme Church where Napoléon Bonaparte is buried, is Paris's most famous landmark: the Eiffel Tower. It was built for the Universal Exhibition in 1889, and despite its astonishing enormity—it stands 1,051 feet (320 m) high—it was only intended as a temporary structure. The tower was quite controversial, but history has silenced its early detractors, and the immense metal structure has been the signature symbol of Paris ever since. Scores of anecdotes are connected to the tower in one way or another, and even the numbers associated with it, because of its sheer size, can themselves be astonishing. For example, the structure is held together by 2.5 million rivets, and even under the windiest conditions, it does not sway more than 4.5 inches (11 cm). On hot days the metal used to construct the tower expands, and the tower grows taller by six inches (15 cm). It weighs about 11,000 tons (10,000 t); about 55 tons (50 t) of that weight is paint.

The view from the top of the tower is worth the inevitable wait for the elevator ride, with the whole city spread out all around. Just one mile due north is the city's other great landmark: the Arc de Triomphe. The triumphal arch was begun in 1806, the year after Napoléon led the French to victory against the Austro-Russian Army at the Battle of Austerlitz. One of the friezes on the side of the arch commemorates this victory, showing French troops drowning the enemy by breaking the ice on a lake.

The arch itself was not, in fact, a great triumph for Napoléon. When he remarried in 1810, after divorcing his childless wife Josephine just a year earlier, he had wanted to lead his new bride through the arch and on to the wedding celebrations at the Louvre Palace. Construction had been delayed, however, and the emperor had to settle for a model of the arch instead. The real structure was not completed until 1836, and four years later Napoléon's body passed under the arch during his own funeral procession. Today, the Arc de Triomphe is the site of the Tomb of the Unknown Soldier, with its everlasting flame. In addition, the arch serves as a focal point for political rallies and major national events, such as the Tour de France.

THE PICTURESQUE STREETS OF PARIS

The official name of the square (actually a circle) where the Arc de Triomphe is located is the place de Charles de Gaulle, named after France's great leader of the late 20th century. This square is also known as l'Étoile (the Star), because no fewer than 12 streets converge there like the points of a star. One of these streets is the broad avenue des Champs-Élysées, which leads in a straight line to the place de la Concorde. On its far side, and in line with the Arc de Triomphe, is the Arc de Triomphe du Carrousel, which stands outside the Louvre.

Opposite from l'Étoile runs the avenue de la Grande Armée, which is in direct line with one of the city's wonderful modern structures, the Grande Arche at La Défense. La Défense is a business and government district complete with shops and restaurants. It is also the site of stunning modern architecture. None is more remarkable than the Grande Arche, a futuristic cube that echoes the designs of the city's other two arches. The Grande Arche is so massive that the entire Notre-Dame Cathedral could fit underneath it.

THE PARISIANS

Throughout its history, Paris has been a melting pot of ethnic groups and cultures. In other world cities, such as New York or

London, immigrant groups have tended to congregate together and build new communities, so that a Chinatown or a Little Italy would develop, and you might feel in those parts of town that you that were indeed in Shanghai or Naples. But the boundaries of the ethnic communities of Paris are not as strongly pronounced as they are elsewhere.

Indeed, it was the very way in which the different ethnic groups blended in Paris that drew many African Americans—writers in particular—to this European city. In the late 1940s and into the 1950s particularly, they came to escape the strongly racist culture of the United States. One such notable author was Richard Wright, who came to Paris in 1947. He has described how in the United States he was always seen as a black man first, and a writer second. In contrast, when he arrived in Paris—a city that has always honored its artists and intellectuals—Wright was welcomed as a writer first.

Nevertheless, Paris too has had its share of racial tensions to deal with, though their issues don't of course have to do with African Americans. Rather, it is North African immigrants who some Parisians view with suspicion or even downright hatred. For many years, France ruled parts of North Africa. It controlled Tunisia and Morocco until 1956, and Algeria until 1962, relinquishing control there only after a long and bloody war. Many people chose to leave these countries and move to France, particularly Paris, to find new opportunities for themselves. As in many countries, however, immigrants have not always been immediately welcomed in Paris.

Today, large numbers of Paris's ethnic communities live in high-rise government housing in the suburbs, rather than in the city itself. One area closer to the city that does show the ethnic diversity of Paris is Belleville. Located about three miles (5 km) northeast of the Louvre, Belleville is home to people from Russia, Poland, Greece, Turkey, North Africa, West Africa, and even Indo-China, where France had fought a colonial war in the early 1950s.

Belleville also has a community of Sephardic Jews, originally from Tunisia. The city's oldest Jewish quarter, however, is in the Marais around the rue des Rosiers. Jewish districts in Paris are much smaller than those found in the United States, because the city's Jewish community suffered terribly under the Nazi occupation of Paris during the Second World War. Nevertheless, it is here where you'll still find Jewish bakeries, bookshops, cafés, and restaurants in among the fashionable cafés and boutiques of the now-expensive Marais district.

Although many immigrant groups have chosen to settle in Paris, the city's ethnic populations are still small compared to other international cities. Of Paris's 2.1 million people, only one percent are Muslim, and just one percent are Jewish. In contrast, about 90 percent are Roman Catholic, two percent are Protestant, and the remaining six percent follow no particular faith.

As a result, Paris is predominantly and unarguably French, with all that this entails. Its citizens are known to be opinionated and argumentative, yet with an old-fashioned belief in courtesy. They are at the same time both conservative and libertarian. Although France is a large nation by European standards and it once controlled a widespread empire, the French remain very insular—just try looking for a non-French wine on the average Parisian wine list, to take just one telling example.

While Parisians may not be interested in foreign wine or food, they have always had a great respect for culture. Artists and intellectuals, and in particular writers, have always played an important part in the life of the city. From its own major talents like Marcel Proust, Gustave Flaubert, Honoré de Balzac, Victor Hugo, and Voltaire to its expatriate writers such as Ernest Hemingway, James Joyce, and Samuel Beckett, Paris has always been a literary city.

○

CHAPTER TWO

Le Grand Siècle

Paris owes its name to a Celtic tribe called the Parisii. They settled on the Île de la Cité in about the year 300 B.C. and called their community Lutetia. Since Lutetia was located in a convenient spot for travelers to cross the River Seine, the Parisii lived by trading as well as fishing. In 52 B.C., the Romans conquered the Parisii and began building on the left bank of the river, where a few Roman remains can still be seen today.

The Roman name for the Celtic people was the Gauls, and the town remained part of Roman Gaul until the late 5th century. At that time, a Germanic tribe called the Franks pushed out the Romans and moved in, marking the beginnings of the modern country of France. Clovis, a Frankish king, made Paris the capital of his kingdom in A.D. 508.

In the 12th century, much of what is recognizably modern Paris was built. There was a permanent food market called Les Halles, which remained until 1969 and is now a modern shopping mall. The foundation stone of Notre-Dame Cathedral was laid in 1163. A fortress was built at the Louvre, and today the remains of its walls are still visible beneath the present-day Louvre Museum.

In 1215, the University of Paris was founded near Notre-Dame. One of its colleges, established in 1253 on the left bank of the river, was the Sorbonne, which quickly became the university's headquarters and remains so today. It was here in 1469 that the first printing works in France was established, and by 1537 it had become the law that a copy of every book published in France must be deposited in the newly built Bibliothèque nationale (National Library).

FRANÇOIS RABELAIS

There is one writer who lived during this time whose name has become part of the language, and not just the French language but the English language, too: François Rabelais. Today, the term *Rabelaisian* describes a way of living or a sense of humor that revels in bawdy excess, which is a little surprising considering that Rabelais was a priest. In fact, just as Casanova was not really a Casanova, Rabelais was not really Rabelaisian. His use of irony allowed him to use salacious humor in order to criticize it and the mentality it betokens.

Rabelais was probably born in 1494, although many of the details about his life are sketchy. He came from a wealthy family and took Holy Orders sometime in his twenties. He studied medicine in Paris and Montpellier before becoming a doctor. Later, he started writing, including the series of books featuring the characters that became associated with him, the giants Gargantua and Pantagruel. The book *Les horribles et épouvantables faits et prouesses du très renommé Pantagruel, roy des Dipsodes (The Horrible and Terrifying Deeds and Words of the Renowned Pantagruel, King of the Dipsodes)* was actually condemned by the Sorbonne for its obscenity, though the fact that the Sorbonne itself received some mocking in the book may have offered some incitement to the school's leaders to denounce it.

Rabelais eventually wrote four books in the series, all of which got him into trouble with the civil authorities. He remained on good terms with the bishops and cardinals, however. He was also popular in the royal courts, where the nobility enjoyed the way the books poked fun at quack doctors and greedy lawyers—always popular subjects for humor. Rabelais died and was buried in Paris in about 1553.

Although Rabelais wrote fantasy stories, the book widely regarded as France's first serious historical novel did not come along until the next century. By then, *le grand siècle* (the great age) was well underway, and this description of the 17th century, and more specifically the reign of the Sun King, Louis XIV, was coined by the writer and philosopher Voltaire, looking back a century later.

OPULENCE GROWS AMONG FRENCH ROYALTY

As scholarship and the arts began to flourish, the French monarchy grew more powerful and wealthy. New palaces were the order of the day, each one more impressive than the last. In 1546, King François I ordered a new palace to be built at the Louvre. Catherine de Médici, widow of King Henri II, began work on a palace in the Tuileries, adjoining the Louvre, in 1559. By 1605, King Henri IV wanted his own new palace, in the Marais district. Before he had a chance to move in, the king was assassinated in 1610. That year, the accession of nine-year-old King Louis XIII, with his mother acting as regent, marked the start of even more prosperous times for France—for the wealthy, at least.

In the first half of the 17th century, even more palaces were being built in Paris. Work began on the Palais du Luxembourg for Marie de Médici in 1615, and in 1632 Cardinal Richelieu was overseeing the conversion of his own mansion into the Palais Cardinal, later to become the Palais-Royal. Then in 1638, the future King Louis XIV was born, a man for whom all the palaces in Paris would not be enough.

Louis XIV was crowned king in 1643, at the age of just four years and eight months. Although he was surrounded by wealth and opulence, it was a lonely childhood for the boy king, who was mostly looked after by servants while others ruled on his behalf. During this time, there was an ongoing battle for power between the royal house, the nobility, the law courts, and the church. Under King Louis XIII, the chief minister, Cardinal Richelieu, had wrestled power away from the law and the nobility to strengthen the grip of the church and the monarchy. The struggle for power boiled over into a series of civil wars known as La Fronde, which took place from 1648 to 1653. Louis XIV was only a boy at the time but it affected him deeply, both physically and emotionally. He felt a permanent resentment against the nobles, the courts of law, and the people in the city of Paris who supported them.

It is not surprising, then, that in 1682 Louis XIV moved the court and the government away from Paris. He had them transferred about 14 miles (23 km) southwest of the city to the wooded countryside at Versailles. His father had ordered construction of a small hunting lodge there in 1623, and the château (castle) had been built in 1631. Under Louis XIV, the gardens were extended and landscaped, and the country's best architects were commissioned to design and build additional wings and the spectacular Hall of Mirrors. Louis XIV invited the nobles of France, long a thorn in the side of the monarchy, to sample his hospitality at Versailles, which they did. He conquered them not in a civil war but by lavishing them with gambling, food, drink, and women.

MOLIÈRE

In 1643, the first year of Louis XIV's reign, a 21-year-old Parisian man named Jean-Baptiste Poquelin was making a decision that would change his own life forever. Poquelin's father was a furnisher appointed to the royal household, and he expected his son would follow in his comfortable footsteps. His son, however, had other ideas and wanted to become an actor, which was considered a disreputable profession. With some friends, he formed a theater company called the Illustre-Théâtre, and he made his stage debut at the new theater at 12 rue Mazarine (the address still exists today, though the building does not). The young man used his newly adopted stage name of Molière.

Molière was not an overnight success. In 1645 he was thrown into prison twice for not paying his debts, and by the end of the year the company had decided to leave Paris and try to make a living by touring in the provinces. The tour was to last 13 years. Evidence suggests that by 1655 the young actor was beginning to turn his hand to writing, as the theater company performed a play in Lyon that was credited to Molière.

By 1658 the company was back in Paris, and things were looking up as the actors were invited to play at the Louvre Palace of the 20-year-old King Louis XIV. They performed a double bill, the second part of which was an original written by Molière, *Le docteur amoureux* (*The Amorous Doctor*). The play, a one-act farce, had been successful on tour, and it was popular in court, too. It appealed to the king enough for him to reward the company with the right to perform at the Petit-Bourbon.

The king's brother Philippe, the Duke of Orléans, soon became the troupe's patron. The royal patronage certainly opened doors for Molière and also enabled the troupe to keep performing. It did not, however, lead to untold wealth and riches. Paris was still a small city, and most people were too poor to spend money on frivolities like the theater. In addition, even with the royal approval, many respectable families regarded actors and prostitutes as members of the same low social caste.

Despite these obstacles, Molière was the driving force behind his theater group and he was undoubtedly the star of the show. He wrote an increasing number of plays for the group to perform, though in part this was because there were precious few good, original plays to chose from. The first play that he both wrote and set in Paris was *Les précieuses ridicules* (usually translated as *The Affected Young Ladies*). It is a farce about two provincial girls, Cathos and Magdelon, who come to Paris and behave in a pretentious way—typical enough materials for a comedy of manners. It satirized the salons then popular in the Marais district, and allowed members of Parisian society to laugh at their own pretensions—their own pride in the city itself being the chief among them: "Paris," as Magdelon declares early in the play, "is the great central office of marvels, the clearing-house of good taste, wit and gallantry" (Bishop 14). The trick to gaining entrée into Paris society has little to do with anything other than participating in "the chitchat of the gallant world" of the city (15), keeping up with the latest news in quips and tunes and love poems: no matter how awful, the most trivial attempt at art must be greeted with ridiculously high-flown approval. So it is when Mascarille, a servant who puts on airs, recites some verses he composed recently—"You stole my heart, engulfing me in grief;/Stop thief! Stop thief! Stop thief! Stop thief! Stop thief!"—the girls respond with the requisite bombast. "That's

Abelard and Héloïse

One of the greatest love stories in French history took place in the early 12th century, and it has been written about ever since. Peter Abelard was born in about 1079, and he became a philosopher and a religious thinker and teacher. He taught in Paris and in 1117 acquired a new student named Héloïse, who was about 20 years his junior. She was also the niece of one of the canons at the church of Notre-Dame, on the site of the present cathedral.

Abelard and Héloïse fell in love, and she went away to Brittany where she secretly had Abelard's child. When she returned to Paris they got married, again in secret. The secret was revealed, however, and a group of Héloïse's relatives attacked Abelard and castrated him. He became a monk, and Héloïse went away to serve as a nun. The two were reunited when Héloïse became the head of a new community of nuns, and Abelard became the abbot. Their letters to each other during their time apart have formed the basis of one of the greatest love stories of all time. They were originally buried together at the nunnery, but in the 19th century their bodies were moved and they now lie side by side in the cemetery at Père-Lachaise in Paris.

the last word in the gallant style!" exclaims Cathos, while Magdelon judiciously acquits it of the charge of being too learned: "Oh, it's a thousand leagues from the pedantic!" (17). The play was a great success—Molière had arrived.

Les précieuses ridicules was probably performed at the Théâtre du Petit-Bourbon, a grand mansion situated next to the royal palace at the Louvre, and could be said to have brought down the house, as the building was demolished soon after the performance. Molière's troupe soon found a new home inside Cardinal Richelieu's Palais-Royal, where all Molière's subsequent plays premiered. Today, the link between Molière and Richelieu still exists. At the junction of the present-day rue Molière and rue de Richelieu, right by the Palais-Royal gardens, stands a fountain that was dedicated to Molière in 1773, the centennial of his death.

By the time of his death Molière had become—and still remains—the best comic playwright that France ever produced. His plays are still performed all around the world, with titles such as *Tartuffe, The Miser, The School for Wives,* and *The Misanthrope* that are still as funny today as they were when Molière created them. His last play was *Le malade imaginaire* (*The Imaginary Invalid*), and with a supreme comic-tragic irony that could have only come from one of his own plays, Molière died while performing on stage, as the curtain came down on play and playwright alike.

Today, Molière's memory lives on at the Comédie-Française, which was founded by Louis XIV in 1680 with the remaining members of Molière's troupe. It still exists, at 2 rue de Richelieu, and performs Molière's plays alongside the best classical and modern dramas. Inside, upstairs, is the armchair into which Molière collapsed and died in that final performance.

JEAN-BAPTISTE RACINE

The other great name in French theater during the 17th century was Jean-Baptiste Racine. Racine is as highly regarded for his tragic plays as Molière was for his comedies, and so in this same short period of history, France produced both of the authors who are still regarded as its two greatest playwrights.

Racine was born in 1639 at La Ferté-Milon in Picardy, about 50 miles (80 km) northeast of Paris. Both his parents died before he was two, and his grandfather died when Racine was nine. His grandmother took him with her to live in the convent at Port-Royal, near Versailles. There, the young Racine studied Greek and Roman literature, works he would eventually use as the basis for many of his own plays. He later studied law at the Collège d'Harcourt in Paris and began to write poetry. For part of this time he was living with his uncle at 7 rue Jacob in St-Germain, which is still an apartment building today.

Racine also began writing plays because, as Molière had shown, it was one of the few ways a writer could make a living at that time. Racine's earnings were not substantial, but a career as a successful dramatist provided enough to live on. Racine's breakthrough came when Molière's highly respected troupe produced two of his early plays at the Palais-Royal: *La Thébaïde ou les frères ennemis* (*The Thebaide or the Enemy Brothers*) in 1664 and *Alexandre le grand* (*Alexander the Great*) in 1665.

Racine's success led not only to professional rivalry between the two chief playwrights of the day, but also to a personal feud. After *Alexandre le grand* met with success at the Palais-Royal, Racine approached a rival theater troupe. It was based at the Hôtel de Bourgogne and was considered to be better at putting on tragedies than Molière's players. Racine wanted them to mount another production of *Alexandre le grand*, which they did, and it opened less than two weeks after Molière's production. Molière naturally saw this as a betrayal of the encouragement he had given the aspiring playwright. If that were not enough, Racine went on to seduce Molière's leading lady and lured her to work at the Hôtel de Bourgogne. From that point on, all of Racine's works were performed there.

In 1667, Racine wrote his first truly great drama, *Andromaque*, a tragedy set in Greece shortly after the Trojan Wars. It bares comparison not only with the great dramas of classical

Greece, but also with some of the works of William Shakespeare that had been first produced in England a century earlier.

Racine continued to use the worlds of ancient Greece and Rome as settings for his dramas, which included *Britannicus* in 1669. This play about the early life of the Emperor Nero has endured as one of Racine's major works, although it was not well received at first. Racine went on to write *Phèdre* in 1677, which was considered then, and now, to be the writer's most mature and accomplished work. For this play, he turned back to Greek mythology and the story of Phèdre, the wife of King Theseus. Having been told that the king is dead, Phèdre turns her attention to Hippolytus, the king's son and her own stepson. When the king reappears and learns what has happened, he has his son killed, while Phèdre subsequently kills herself.

Although his plays were tragedies, Racine was far from being a tragic figure himself. His success brought him invitations to the same salons in the fashionable Marais district that Molière attended, and both writers were regulars at a cabaret called La Pomme de Pin (The Pine-Comb). This institution had been operating since about 1400, and Rabelais had also been a frequent visitor. It was located at place du Parvis-Notre-Dame, which is now the Hôtel-Dieu Hospital.

After Racine's success with *Phèdre*, he put down his pen and never wrote another play, apart from a few minor pieces. In 1677, Racine was offered the job of official historian to King Louis XIV, a position that must have been extremely tempting and a great honor for the playwright. It involved Racine accompanying the king to many great occasions, and even onto the battlefield to chronicle the king's military campaigns. During this period of his life, Racine lived at 17 rue Visconti, very close to his earlier home with his uncle at 7 rue Jacob. In 1699, he died in this house, which is still a private home today, and was buried in the church of Saint-Étienne-du-Mont in nearby Place Ste-Geneviève.

JEAN DE LA FONTAINE

Early in his career, Racine had become friends with the great French writer Jean de la Fontaine. De la Fontaine was born in 1621 in the Champagne region of France, near Reims. Like his father before him, de la Fontaine became an inspector of the local forests and waterways, but he also spent time in nearby Paris. De la Fontaine's interest in rural matters influenced his poetry and his prose writings, and he was widely celebrated for his fables featuring animal characters, rather in the manner of the more famous Aesop. The fables were incredibly popular and there were numerous collections published, the first of which was printed in 1668.

Later in his life, de la Fontaine was known to be a visitor to Le Procope. When it opened in 1686, Le Procope became Paris's first café and it quickly became the haunt of the city's writers and artists. There, de la Fontaine would have occasionally met with Racine and Molière, among others. Le Procope still exists today at the same address, 13 rue de l'Ancienne-Comédie. Today, however, it is a restaurant rather than a café, and the present décor dates from the 18th century rather than the 17th. De la Fontaine died in Paris in 1695.

COMTESSE DE LA FAYETTE AND MADAME DE SÉVIGNÉ

A notable contemporary of de la Fontaine's, but writing in a very different genre, was the Comtesse (Countess) de la Fayette. In 1678, she wrote what is thought to be the first significant French novel. Madame de la Fayette had been born in Paris in 1634, and through the socialite and prolific letter-writer Madame de Sévigné she met the Comte (Count) de la Fayette. The couple married in 1655, though they separated just four years later.

The comtesse lived in both the royal and the literary worlds, for in France politics and the arts have always been closely linked. She wrote two books that were light romances before starting work on a more serious historical novel, which she set in the 16th century. In 1678, *La princesse de Clèves* (*The Princess of Clèves*) was published. This novel was published anonymously, however, because it dealt with subjects never before broached in literary works—the passionate thoughts of a young married woman toward another man. The book was the first French—indeed, European—novel to treat such matters seriously, portraying the characters as rounded human beings with feelings and problems, rather than as cardboard characters who were either good or evil, virtuous or lecherous, ugly or beautiful, as they often were in the romances and picaresque narratives that predated the novel.

The comtesse died in Paris in 1693, but the world in which she moved can still be glimpsed today by visiting the place des Vosges in the Marais district. This elegant square is still surrounded by grand mansions, although some have been converted for use as hotels and others remain private residences. One such private residence, at number 1 places des Vosges, is the Hôtel de Coulanges. It is where the comtesse's matchmaker, Madame de Sévigné, had been born on February 6, 1626.

Madame de Sévigné's full title was Marie de Rabutin-Chantal, the Marquise de Sévigné. The numerous letters she wrote—more than 1,500 of them, mostly to her daughter in Provence—paint a vivid portrait of the life of Parisian gentry in the 17th century. They are among the most famous letters in French literary history, describing the salons where educated and artistic people gathered to discuss the topics of the day. The Comtesse de la Fayette regularly attended the salons, as did Molière and his rival Racine.

VERSAILLES

From 1682 onward, however, there was only one place to be and that was the lavish new royal palace at Versailles. If the mansions of the Marais were impressive, then the new home of the Louis XIV was overwhelming. Approximately 30,000 people are said to have worked on the project, and when it was occupied there were about 20,000 servants, government workers, maintenance men, and others all working at Versailles and living nearby. Today, Versailles is a sizeable town of 90,000 people, and the château is easily reached by train from central Paris, making it a very popular day trip from the capital.

A visit to Versailles is a must for Parisian visitors, and not merely as an entertaining day visit. Its size and opulence can barely be imagined. The single most spectacular sight is the Hall of Mirrors. The hall is 233 feet (71 m) long and lined with countless mirrors and crystal chandeliers, making the room appear to stretch away to the horizon. It was in this room that the Treaty of Versailles was signed in 1919, when the United States, Great Britain, France, and Italy formally negotiated a peaceful conclusion to the First World War.

To see the features at Versailles—its opera house, royal chapel, and vast formal gardens with spectacular water displays—is to understand not only the wealth of the French royal family at that time, but also to understand why, less than a hundred years after the end of *le grand siècle*, there was to be a popular uprising: the French Revolution.

CHAPTER THREE

The Age of Enlightenment

The period between the end of *le grand siècle* and the start of the French Revolution is known as the Age of Enlightenment, an epoch of development in science, philosophy, and the arts in which reason, polish, urbanity, and classicism ruled culture. In France, however, the citizens were also slowly becoming enlightened about the lavish lifestyle and excessive wealth of their rulers. The rich were getting richer and the poor were not only getting poorer, but their population was increasing as well.

To understand Paris in the 18th century, one must understand the two faces of the city. On one hand were the large mansions of the Marais and Montmartre, the salons where witty and prosperous people met to chat about the issues of the day. On the other hand, however, there were the city's dreadful slums where people lived in appalling poverty and degradation. They were not idling time away in witty conversations; they were using their wits to survive.

The problem of poverty, beggars, and vagrants was not a new one for Paris. In 1596, there had been so many vagrants living on the streets that they were given 24 hours to leave the city. If they chose not to leave, the vagrants faced death by hanging or strangulation, with no thought of a trial. These threats did not work for long, however. By the middle of the 17th century, Paris had an estimated 400,000 residents and about 10 percent of them were vagrants. While members of the nobility were building palaces all over the city, about 10,000 Parisians were living in a kind of vagrants' prison.

By the start of the Age of Enlightenment, during an especially fierce winter in 1708–1709, it was reported that more than 2,500 infants were abandoned in doorways, most left to die and be thrown into mass graves. So bad were conditions in parts of the city, especially around the marketplace of Les Halles, that the authorities ordered the slums to be flattened in the mid-17th century. By this time the city had its first police force, paid for by King Louis XIV, with officers who wore blue uniforms to enable people to identify them as they patrolled the city streets.

By the dawn of the 18th century, the city was certainly developing. It not only had a police force, but it also had a streetlight system, a daily newspaper, a public bus service, a postal service, theaters, hospitals, and even the first stone-arched bridge across the River Seine. This all appeared very progressive, and indeed enlightened, but all was not well in the city. In addition to the problems of poverty, King Louis XIV seemed determined to wage endless wars against the Dutch, the Spanish, the British, the Italians, and in fact, most of Europe.

Louis XIV reigned for 72 years, but for half that time his country was at war, at incredible cost to the royal coffers, which had to be replenished by increased taxes and unscrupulous financial dealings. When the sun finally went down on the Sun King at Versailles in 1715, his death was not greatly mourned. His crown passed to his great-grandson, Louis XV, who was only five years old. For that reason, a regent—Philippe II, the Duke of Orléans—ruled on Louis XV's behalf until 1723. From that time on, the country descended further into corruption and chaos, under both the regent and later the new king.

Philippe was a notorious man-about-town, widely known as a man who preferred gambling to government. He became involved in a get-rich-quick scheme that encouraged wealthy Parisians to invest in Louisiana and other French colonies. These investments were supposed to make them richer, but everyone lost money. As a result, Philippe was as unpopular with the well-to-do Parisians as he was with those who were poverty stricken.

When Louis reached his maturity and fully took over the crown, he was no more successful than Louis XIV had been. He continued to wage wars and took little interest in what was going on at home. He took more notice of his various wives and mistresses, who were thought by many to interfere with the running of the country. This made him even less popular with all levels of society. He had initially been nicknamed *le Bien-Aimé* (the Well-Beloved) king, but the feeling did not last and by the time of his death at Versailles in 1774, he was one of the least-beloved rulers in French history. He reigned for almost 60 years, on top of his predecessor's reign of 72 years—a very long time for a country to be governed by two unpopular and mainly ineffective monarchs.

VOLTAIRE

If it was a bad time, politically and socially, for the country, it was a good time for a satirical writer like Voltaire to be alive. Voltaire was born in Paris in 1694, his real name being François-Marie Arouet. He attended the Jesuit college of Louis Le Grand, which still exists today at 123 rue St-Jacques. The college was founded in 1550, and it has a distinguished list of literary students, such as Molière, Charles-Pierre Baudelaire, and Victor Hugo. More recently, many leading French politicians—including former presidents Georges Pompidou, Valéry Giscard d'Estaing, and Jacques Chirac—have attended the school.

It was while attending this college that Voltaire quickly gained a love of literature and the theater, as well as a reputation for being a great wit—a characteristic that would stay with him all his life. It would also constantly get him into trouble, an early example being a piece he wrote that poked fun at France's regent, the Duke of Orléans, for which Voltaire spent almost a year in the Bastille prison in 1717.

While he was in the Bastille, Voltaire wrote the first of his tragic plays, *Oedipe* (*Oedipus*), which was a great hit when it was performed in 1718. Voltaire also wrote poetry and essays, and he was quickly becoming well known in the city. Despite this, many people found his ideas provocative. For example, Voltaire was anti-Christian in a country were most people were Christian, and he believed that religion was the cause of many of the world's evils.

Less than 10 years after leaving the Bastille, Voltaire found himself in trouble again. In 1726, a Parisian nobleman, the Chevalier de Rohan, made fun of Voltaire's pen name and a violent argument ensued. The nobleman was injured and Voltaire found himself returning to the Bastille. On his release, he was taken to Calais and exiled to England.

Voltaire had long been interested in England, which was perceived as a land of greater freedom and tolerance than France. Voltaire had begun to learn English earlier in his life, but he mastered it more fully during almost two years of exile. This allowed him to read the works of English writers and philosophers, since at this time literature was not as widely translated as it is today. While in England Voltaire met many writers, including the Irishman Jonathan Swift, the author of *Gulliver's Travels*, who in many ways was a kind of Irish Voltaire.

Voltaire was allowed to return to Paris in 1728. Back in France, Voltaire returned to writing drama with renewed enthusiasm, having been greatly influenced in England by the works of William Shakespeare. Not all Voltaire's plays were successful, but by this point Voltaire was wealthy enough not to worry, since he had invested his earlier earnings wisely. Voltaire was independent financially, but he was just as independent as a thinker. In 1734, he published a slim volume called *Lettres philosophiques*, which dared to suggest among other things that mankind would develop more by pursuing the arts and sciences than it would by pursuing religion. At the same time, it promoted religious tolerance and advocated civil liberties of a kind that the average French citizen was not allowed. A warrant was issued for Voltaire's arrest, and this time he took refuge in the château belonging to his lover, the Marquise du Châtelet, in the Champagne region not far from Paris. The couple is known to have also stayed at the Hôtel Lambert, 2 rue St-Louis-en-l'Île, while Voltaire was working on *La Henriade*, an epic poem about King Henri IV, which was published in 1728.

As Voltaire continued to write, he remained both prolific and provocative, producing poetry, fiction, and essays. He also wrote plays, some of which were performed at the Comédie-Française. As time passed, Voltaire's link with Paris continued. In 1739, for example, he protested the proposed Fontaine des Quatre Saisons (Fountain of the Four Seasons), as he said the street was too narrow and a fountain should not be flat against a wall but should be able to be seen from all sides. Today, visitors can see the fountain at 57–59 rue de Grenelle and decide whether they agree with Voltaire.

After the death of his friend the Marquise du Châtelet in 1749, Voltaire lived in various places but finally settled in Ferney, now called Ferney-Voltaire in his honor, near the French border with Switzerland. There he produced more works, and in 1759 he published the novel for which he is probably best known, *Candide*. The belief of the naive character Candide, who travels the world having adventures, is that everything is always for the best no matter what indignities and sufferings he encounters. He maintains this belief until the end, when he realizes that the best thing is, in fact, to stay home and "cultivate one's own garden," enjoying life's simple pleasures.

Meanwhile, the theater continued to excite Voltaire, and it was this that brought him back to Paris in 1778, after an absence of some 28 years. On March 30, his play *Irène* was performed to a rapturous audience, delighted to see the 84-year-old grand old man—and perennial renegade—of French literature back in his home city. The excitement proved too much for the already frail Voltaire, who died in Paris two months later at what is now number 27 on the quai Voltaire.

Although Voltaire was taken away from Paris for burial, his body was returned after the French Revolution. Today his tomb can be seen in the Panthéon, where the great and the good of the city of Paris are now buried. This building at place du Panthéon was opened in 1789 as a church in honor of Saint Geneviève, the patron saint of Paris. It was built by King Louis XV, as thanks for his recovery from a serious case of gout. The building was meant to resemble the Panthéon in Rome, but the plans changed in the 45 years that passed between the king's vow and the eventual opening. In 1791, it was turned into a place of honor for the great citizens who had fought for French liberty before and during the Revolution. Since then, many notable figures have been buried there, including Émile Zola, Victor Hugo, Jean-Jacques Rousseau, Louis Braille, and Marie Curie.

Although his tomb is at the Panthéon, Voltaire's heart is in the Bibliothèque National de France (National Library of France) on rue de Richelieu near the Palais-Royal. It's contained in the pedestal of a statue of Voltaire, in the library's Salon d'Honneur (Room of Honor), which during his lifetime surely the writer could never have imagined happening.

MONTESQUIEU

Voltaire was the most notable writer of this period, but he was certainly not the only writer in Paris. A contemporary of Voltaire's was the grandly named Charles-Louis de Secondat, Baron de la Brède et de Montesquieu, more commonly known just by the name of Montesquieu. He was born in 1689, five years before Voltaire, and came from a respectable middle-class military family in the wine-producing region of Bordeaux. His mother owned vineyards, and the family was wealthy but not aristocratic. At the age of 11, Montesquieu was sent away to a school near Paris and then graduated with a degree in law from the University of Bordeaux. He practiced law in Paris for a while, but then he returned to Bordeaux when his father died in

1713. Montesquieu married a wealthy woman and inherited more money and a seat in the Bordeaux Parliament when one of his uncles died. All in all, a fairly comfortable upbringing.

It was a great surprise, then, when in 1721 he published his first book, *Lettres persanes* (*Persian Letters*). It was published anonymously, but the author's identity was soon known. If it was a surprise that someone with no literary background at all should suddenly publish a book at the age of 32, when his life was one of the utmost respectability, the subject matter of the book was even more of a surprise. It was in the form of a collection of letters written by two Persian travelers in France, commenting on French—in particular Parisian—society, mostly in unflattering and satirical terms. It poked fun at the excesses of former King Louis XIV, who had died only six years earlier. It was also critical of the Catholic Church at a time when most people in France were Catholic, and Montesquieu frequently compared the Christian and Islamic religions, which was not always flattering to the Christian point of view. It was an astonishing book to come from an unknown writer at that time, not long after the great Voltaire himself had been imprisoned for some of his satirical writing.

The book was a great success, and in the year following its publication Montesquieu moved to Paris in order to further his surprising new career as an author. He was soon attending the literary salons of the day and even moving in royal circles. Despite the criticisms that writers such as Montesquieu and Voltaire made of the royal way of life, their popularity and importance meant that they were courted by everyone, including the very people they ridiculed. It was a fine line, however, and Voltaire often found himself in trouble for overstepping it.

It seemed that Montesquieu, on the other hand, could do no wrong. He was socially ambitious and soon after arriving in Paris he was lobbying to join l'Académie française (French Academy). Cardinal Richelieu had formed this distinguished body, and its members had the task of compiling a French dictionary. Membership was limited to just 40 prominent writers and scholars, who met at the Louvre. Today l'Académie française is still part of Parisian society, and its members meet at the Institut de France at 23 quai de Conti. One of their tasks is to preserve the purity of the French language, partly by discouraging the use of too many modern words and foreign phrases that have been infiltrating the language. For example, because French had no equivalent word for the English word *weekend*, French people started using the English word and talking about *le weekend.* This kind of language has the members of the Académie throwing up their hands in despair and endeavoring to find a suitable French word to fill the gap.

To be elected to the Académie has always been considered a

The National Library

The Bibliothèque nationale de France (National Library of France) has two sites within the city. The original building is called the "site Richelieu" and can be found at 58 rue de Richelieu. In 1537, it was decreed that one copy of every book published in France must be given to the library. In addition to the books, the library now holds manuscripts, maps, photographs, musical scores, and other items. It also contains the Mazarin Gallery, which can be viewed when special exhibitions are on display, and the Museum of Medals and Antiques, which is open daily in the afternoons.

In 1998, the National Library's collection of 11 million books was moved to a new branch of the National Library in Bercy, called the "site François-Mitterand." This new site, just east of the city center, has an impressive four seven-story modern buildings. Each building is set in the corner of a rectangle and in the shape of four open books, facing inward. The design has been as much criticized as it has been praised, as is the way with modern buildings. The library is open to the public but books must be requested a day in advance.

great honor, and membership is still restricted to only 40 people. For Montesquieu, to be elected would be a sign that he had truly arrived in Parisian society. First, though, a vacancy had to arise, which usually meant waiting for one of the existing members to die. In 1727, Montesquieu's chance arose. With the help of strong lobbying from one of the prominent salons he attended, Montesquieu's wish was granted and he became a member of the Académie.

Three months later, he set off on a grand tour of Europe. Montesquieu wanted the honor of being elected, but not the responsibility that went with it. He did, however, write an account of his travels through Austria, Hungary, Italy, Germany, Holland, and England, where he lived for 18 months. Upon returning to France three years after setting off, Montesquieu decided to concentrate on literature and returned to his family home in Bordeaux, where he spent the next two years writing.

Montesquieu kept in touch with Parisian society and attended meetings of the Académie, while also producing works on the English Constitution and the Roman Empire. He then embarked on his major work, a remarkable study of law and politics that would eventually be published in 31 volumes in 1748 under the impressive title of *De l'esprit des loix, ou du rapport que les loix doivent avoir avec la constitution de chaque gouvernement, les moeurs, le climat, la religion, le commerce, etc.* It was translated under the more abbreviated title of *The Spirit of Laws,* and it investigated the advantages and disadvantages of different types of government, including both a monarchy and a republic. Not long after the work's publication, France would switch from one type of government to the other.

DENIS DIDEROT

Just as l'Académie française had busied itself preparing a French dictionary in the 17th century, the first French encyclopedia was being compiled in the 18th century. The work exemplified the very systematic search for knowledge that the Age of

Enlightenment is known for. The man behind this encyclopedia was a writer and philosopher named Denis Diderot.

Diderot was born in the town of Langres, almost 200 miles (322 km) southeast of Paris, in 1713. He moved to Paris in 1729 to attend college, and afterward stayed on in the city, scraping together a living as a writer and teacher. In doing so he was joining the ranks of musicians, scientists, actors, and writers who gravitated to Paris from the provinces in order to make their names, often living in picturesque bohemian poverty before breaking through. In 1745, a publisher invited Diderot to translate and edit an encyclopedia that had been written by Ephraim Chambers and published in England. Diderot agreed to what would grow into a massive project. During part of the time he worked on it, Diderot lived at 3 rue de l'Estrapade, which gives a good view over the Panthéon.

As Diderot put more effort into the encyclopedia, the project grew and grew. He began commissioning essays by prominent French writers including Voltaire and Montesquieu, whose provocative views are not what modern readers would expect to find in an encyclopedia today. This encyclopedia eventually expanded into 17 volumes, with an additional 11 volumes of illustrations.

Diderot's encyclopedia first appeared in 1751, but it was not well received by the church or the royal court. In 1759, the first ten volumes were banned, and Voltaire offered to help have the remaining volumes published outside France. Despite the ban, Diderot continued to have the encyclopedias secretly published in France, and in 1772 the final volume with illustrations and supplements came out. Diderot continued to publish his own works of philosophy and fiction alongside working on the encyclopedia. Diderot died in 1784 and was laid to rest in the Église St-Roch (Church of St-Roch) on the rue St-Honoré. Several of Diderot's works were published posthumously.

Paris for Diderot was to be honored as a city that encouraged the life of the mind by putting aspiring thinkers and artists in touch with one another. In the 1740s and 50s Diderot regularly associated with such notable figures as Jean-Jacques Rousseau, Jean Le Rond d'Alembert, and Etienne Bonnot de Condillac—a writer, a mathematician, and a psychologist, respectively. Rousseau writes in his *Confessions* of the way the members of the little circle worked together:

> I spoke to Diderot about Condillac and his work; and introduced them to one another. They were born to agree, and they did so. Diderot induced Durand the bookseller to take the Abbé's manuscript, and that great metaphysician received from his first book ... a hundred crowns, which perhaps he would not have earned but for me. As we all lived in widely different quarters, the three of us met once a week at the Palais-Royal, and went to dine together at the Hôtel du Panier-Fleuri. These little weekly dinners must have pleased Diderot; for though he almost always failed to keep his appointments, even with women, he never missed one of them. (*Rousseau* 324–25)

Rousseau was later to leave Paris, vowing never again to live in the city; that Diderot continued to value what Paris offered in terms of culture and refinement is reflected in the lightly veiled rebuke of Rousseau that he wrote into his play *Fils naturel* (*The Natural Son*): "I appeal to your heart: ask it, and it will tell you that the good man lives in society, and only the bad man lives alone" (qtd. in Wilson 255).

PIERRE-AUGUSTIN CARON DE BEAUMARCHAIS

One writer from this era whose work lives on today, though his name is hardly known, is Pierre-Augustin Caron de Beaumarchais. Beaumarchais wrote two plays that were subsequently turned into operas. Today these operas—*The Barber of Seville* and *The Marriage of Figaro*—are still among the most popular on the stage.

Beaumarchais was born in Paris in 1732. He was the son of a watchmaker, and he himself became a watchmaker to King

Louis XV. Beaumarchais had an inventive mind and patented several new watchmaking techniques. Others also used similar techniques however, and this resulted in a series of court actions, not all of which were in Beaumarchais's favor.

Beaumarchais was a jack of all trades. He was also a talented musician and taught King Louis XV's daughters to play the harp. Subsequently, Louis XV and later Louis XVI employed him as a spy, and he was sent to Germany and England on secret missions. He also went to America to sell arms that he'd bought to the American colonists in their fight for independence from France's rival, Great Britain. Beaumarchais also spent time as a financial speculator and made quite a bit of money. In addition, Beaumarchais was a literary enthusiast and he was the first to publish a complete collection of the works of Voltaire after Voltaire's death in 1778.

Beaumarchais wrote several plays and memoirs, but he made his name with the two comedies that have proved eternally popular. He wrote the play *The Barber of Seville* in 1775, which Italian composer Gioacchino Rossini converted into an opera in 1815. In 1784 Beaumarchais wrote another play, *The Marriage of Figaro*. Almost immediately afterward, renowned Austrian composer Wolfgang Amadeus Mozart turned it into an opera, which was produced in 1786. Despite Beaumarchais's closeness to France's monarchs, the plays dealt with the abuse of power by the aristocracy. Both plays were censored, and *The Marriage of Figaro* was at first banned by King Louis XVI.

Paris has several sites associated with Beaumarchais. One is the École Militaire (Military Academy), which Louis XV wanted to build in the 1770s. The king was looking for ways of financing the academy without digging into the royal coffers. Beaumarchais came up with two ideas: to run a lottery and to place a tax on playing cards. Today, the École Militaire stands today at 1 place Joffre, but visits are by appointment only.

Given his literary fame and association with nobility, Beaumarchais lived, naturally, in the fashionable mansions of the Marais. For a time he resided at the Hôtel des Ambassadeurs de

Hollande, 47 rue Vieille-du-Temple, and it was while living here that he wrote *The Marriage of Figaro*. Further along the same street at number 12 is the Hôtel Caron de Beaumarchais, which dates back to the time of Beaumarchais and has some displays about the writer, although there is no direct link between the writer and the hotel.

The playwright later moved into a grand mansion at what is now numbers 2–20 boulevard Beaumarchais, although the building no longer stands. What does stand is his statue, at the junction of rue St-Antoine and rue des Tournelles. It is appropriately situated between the Marais and the site of the Bastille, for, like Voltaire, Beaumarchais was another writer who sampled both the salons of the Marais and the cells of the prison. He was thrown in jail in 1792, after the Revolution, because of his immense wealth, although he was released after one of his former mistresses interceded on his behalf. He died in 1799, and his last resting place is in the cemetery at Père-Lachaise.

Beaumarchais's life bridged the gap between the old France, governed by the monarchy, and the new France, with a new constitution and a new republic. The events that brought these changes produced one of the bloodiest revolutions Europe had as yet seen, and it was about to begin.

CHAPTER | **FOUR**

Revolution

"It was the best of times, it was the worst of times." The famous paradoxical opening of British author Charles Dickens's novel *A Tale of Two Cities* sums up life in Paris at the time of the Revolution. The book was published in 1859, only about 70 years after the Revolution's main events took place. The fact that Great Britain's greatest living writer chose to tackle the French Revolution in fiction reflects the impact and significance of what had happened. It was as dramatic as the American War of Independence had been just a few years earlier on the other side of the Atlantic. The world order was changing.

It had been the best of times for the French aristocracy, as well as members of the royal family who were living in shameless luxury in the palace at Versailles. It had been the worst of times, however, for the ordinary French people who lived at the opposite end of the social scale. Vast numbers of French people lived in total poverty, and their numbers were on the rise. By the late 18th century, France had Europe's largest population. While many of those people were starving, their rulers lived lives of unimaginable luxury.

For those who felt sympathy for the plight of the poor, the

Revolution could be seen as the best of times. They had hope that a more just society would be created in the future. So many horrific things happened during the Revolution, however, that there was no hesitation in calling it the worst of times, too.

When Dickens's novel begins in 1775, Britain and France are undergoing similar periods of social unrest. In France, Louis XVI had been on the throne one year, and Napoléon Bonaparte was just six years old. Meanwhile, across the Atlantic a war of independence was just beginning in Britain's American colonies. The French granted sizeable loans to the American colonies to help them in their struggle. The resulting debts further drained the nation's resources, which were already strained thanks to the warmongering of Louis XIV and the ineffective rule of Louis XV.

THE SITUATION WORSENS

France's financial situation worsened over the next few years, and eventually hungry and angry crowds of people began marching at Versailles. Troops were called out to deal with the crowds, and many people were killed. Some of the protests were about the increasing price of bread, which many poor people could no longer afford. The queen, Marie-Antoinette, is said to have asked what the people were complaining about. When told that it was the price of bread, she replied: "Let them eat cake." She herself was so surrounded by wealth, by food, by a choice of everything, that she could not—or did not care to—conceive of a world where people were unable to afford to eat bread, let alone eat cake. Whether it is true or not, the remark has gone down in history and the mobs protesting in the Paris streets certainly believed that it had been said. Her arrogance and ignorance only angered those in need the more.

At the same time, other levels of society were complaining about the royal rule. In defiance of the royal household, the National Assembly was established in 1789 to allow people more say in how their country was run. The assembly claimed the right to levy taxes, taking this away from the king. In response, the king took away the assembly's meeting hall. The assembly then met at a tennis court at Versailles and declared that it would continue to meet until a new French constitution was prepared.

The royal army was becoming increasingly concerned at the turn of events, torn between loyalty to the king and being asked to turn against their own people. Foreign armies were drafted to protect the palace at Versailles and the palaces in Paris itself, an action that only inflamed the people of the city even more. Protests turned into riots, and in turn the riots resulted in the most significant symbolic event of the whole Revolution: the storming of the Bastille.

The infamous Bastille prison had first been built in about 1370 as part of the city's walled fortifications and as a royal palace. In the 17th century, it was turned into the French state prison and became particularly hated because it was where political prisoners were held indefinitely without trial, in very harsh conditions.

As a result, the Bastille prison stood as a symbol of the monarchy's absolute power. On July 14, 1789, the people of Paris, with help from the royal army, stormed the Bastille. The mob of several hundred quickly secured the release of the prisoners and hanged the prison governor. The attack was quickly followed by the Bastille's destruction, as the mob tore it down.

So important was the storming of the Bastille that July 14 is now a national holiday in France, Bastille Day. It signifies the end of the old order and the beginning of the new. Despite this, the storming was more of a symbol than anything else, because there were only seven prisoners inside it at the time and none of them were political prisoners.

Today the Bastille is a large square, a metro station, and the name for an area east of the Marais. Nothing remains of the Bastille prison, although some paving stones on the west side of the wide place de la Bastille mark where the building's eight original towers once stood. In the center of the place de la Bastille is the 171-foot (52-m) high bronze monument called the Colonne de Juillet (July Column), which is topped by a golden statue known as the genius of liberty. The statue commemorates later uprisings that occurred in 1830 and 1848, for 1789 was not the only French revolution, but merely the first and most significant.

THE MAN IN THE IRON MASK

Several writers had been imprisoned in the Bastille, among them Voltaire and the Marquis de Sade. They were not the prison's only celebrated inmates, however. The Bastille was also a source of inspiration of other authors, including 19th century writer Alexandre Dumas. Dumas wrote about an inmate known as "the man in the iron mask." In truth, the inmate probably did not wear an iron mask. It was more likely that he wore a black cloth mask, which was commonly used to hide the identities of prisoners, but "iron mask" makes for a better story.

In either case, the inmate known as "the man in the iron mask" was a mysterious political prisoner who died in the Bastille in 1703. There are various contenders for who the man might have been, including suggestions that he was an English nobleman or the older brother of King Louis XIV who held some shameful or potentially damaging secret. This latter notion was put forward initially by Voltaire, and it formed the basis of the later novel by Dumas. It is one of the more unlikely scenarios. Even less likely is the theory that the man in the iron mask was actually the playwright Molière.

Although many of the details about this inmate are unclear, some facts are known. Sometime before 1681, a man was imprisoned in a place called Pignerol in what is now the Piedmont region of northwest Italy. Permanently masked, he was moved around various prisons before reaching the Bastille in September 1698. He died five years later and was buried nearby, his gravestone only saying that his name was Marchioly and that his age was "about 45." If accurate, this would mean he had spent almost all of his adult life in prison, his identity kept a secret—a mystery indeed.

So what are the clues to the possible identity of this man of mystery? One possibility was a man named Matthioli, a name that does bear a resemblance to the name of Marchioly on the tombstone, which could be a corruption. Matthioli was a minister to the Duke of Mantua and had been secretly negotiating on the duke's behalf to sell part of Piedmont to the French for a large sum of money. It is said that Matthioli betrayed the duke's dealings, and was imprisoned as a result. On the other hand, it is also believed that Matthioli died in 1694, making it impossible for him to be the man in the iron mask.

The most likely man in the iron mask is thought to have been Eustache Dauger. Dauger was a valet to a French finance

The American Connection

Benjamin Franklin, who helped to draw up the American Declaration of Independence and was one of its original signers, was no stranger to Paris. He came to the city in 1776 to try to raise support, and cash, for the American cause. He knew he would get a sympathetic hearing in Paris, because there had never been any love lost between the French and the British. Franklin stayed at what was then the Hôtel d'Entragues, 2–4 rue de l'Université, in the heart of St-Germain. The building still stands today, although it is now a block of private apartments rather than a hotel.

Franklin returned to Paris in 1783, this time to help organize the signing of the Treaty of Paris. It was the document that formalized the independence of the 13 American colonies from the British and acknowledged the United States of America as a free nation. Few American visitors who tour the Left Bank of Paris today are aware that this historic document was signed in what was then the Hôtel d'York at 56 rue Jacob, also in the St-Germain district, less than a block away from the former Hôtel d'Entragues.

minister, Nicolas Fouquet, who himself would eventually be imprisoned for embezzlement. Dauger was thrown in prison in 1669 at the order of one of Louis XIV's ministers, Louvois. The reason for his imprisonment is unknown, but it may well have been that in his position as valet to a disreputable finance minister, Dauger may have learned too much about dubious goings-on in the royal household and the royal treasury. If this is the case, the secrets he learned must have been quite shameful to warrant his masking and imprisonment. However, it has created yet another enduring story about the hated Bastille prison.

PIERRE CHODERLOS DE LACLOS

One writer who would have surely seen the inside of the Bastille, had it not been torn down before his arrest, is Pierre Choderlos de Laclos. Laclos was born in Amiens, about 80 miles (129 km) north of Paris, in 1741. He came from a family of French nobility, and went to military school and pursued a career in the army before becoming a writer. He had only published some minor works, including some poetry, when he had his greatest success with a book that is still widely read today, *Les liaisons dangereuses* (*Dangerous Liaisons*).

Les liaisons dangereuses was published in 1782, several years before the height of the French Revolution. The book was an astonishing success, as it was something entirely new. The book was written in the form of a series of letters by different characters. The epistolary form of the novel, and the particular perspective on characters' psychology that the form helps to channel, link it to Samuel Richardson's massive novel *Clarissa*, which tells a similar story of virtue and seduction. *Les liaisons dangereuses* was a forerunner of the great French novels of the 19th century by writers such as Honoré de Balzac and Émile Zola, who were also fascinated by the psychological makeup of their characters.

The book's central character, Valmont, is a notorious rake who is engaged in seducing Présidente de Tourvel at the start of the novel. He is taunted and aided by turns by Madame de

Merteuil, who wants him to help her cuckold an ex-lover of hers (and ex-rival of Valmont's) named Gercourt by compromising the virtue of Gercourt's young bride-to-be, Cécile Volanges, a girl of fifteen. The reward, for both, will be Gercourt's foolishness in the eyes of Paris society, as Merteuil writes in the second letter of the book: "Let us prove to [Gercourt] that he is a mere fool; no doubt he will be one day—that is not what troubles me—but it would be amusing to have him begin by being one. How it will delight us to hear him boasting on the morning after (for he will boast); and then, if you once mould this girl, it would be very unlucky if Gercourt, like anybody else, does not become the talk of Paris" (68). Valmont and Merteuil delight in their schemes of corruption, and so the novel is in part an exposure of the decadence of high society at that time—a popular subject with writers and readers alike. It is still a popular subject today, and the book was adapted into a successful play and has been filmed several times, including versions by Roger Vadim and Milos Forman.

Laclos never wrote anything else that came close to the success of his most famous book, and he later rejoined the army. Like many authors at this time, Laclos straddled various levels of society and was part of the nobility while at the same time criticizing it. One of his later books was very critical of the French Army, and he lost his commission as an officer as a result of it, which is perhaps just as well as it happened on the eve of the Revolution. Laclos later became secretary to the Duke of Orléans and was imprisoned and almost executed in 1793. He survived, however, and joined the army yet again, and was successful under the post-revolutionary French leader, Napoléon. Laclos was promoted to the rank of general by Napoléon himself, and he died from a fever while on active service in 1803.

THE REVOLUTION CONTINUES

After the storming of the Bastille in July 1789, the Revolution moved ahead rapidly. Feudalism was abolished on August 4, and the Declaration of the Rights of Man and the Citizen was adopted on August 26. In October, the royal family was brought from the palace at Versailles and imprisoned in the palace at the Tuileries. In June 1791, the queen and her children escaped and just one year later, mobs of rioting citizens invaded the Tuileries Palace and seized the king. In September 1792, the monarchy was finally officially abolished, and the First French Republic was proclaimed.

This was not the end of the Revolution, but in fact was the start of a period known as the Terrors. It was a time when thousands of people were put to death on the guillotine. Many people seized this lawless time to take bloody revenge on their enemies, denouncing them to the authorities, with or without evidence. In January 1793, King Louis XVI was found guilty of treason and executed. In October of that year, Queen Marie-Antoinette also paid the price, and she was sentenced to visit "Madame Guillotine." The cell in which she was held can be seen at the Conciergerie, a 14th century Gothic palace that was used for part of the time as a prison, and is now open to the public.

It was July 1794 before the Terrors ended and the first French Revolution came to a close. France no longer had a king, but it no longer had a strong ruler either. Within a few years, though, it would have one of the strongest leaders any European nation had ever produced: Napoléon Bonaparte. He seized power in 1799 to become France's first consul, and in 1804 he was crowned emperor. Napoléon took France forward onto the battlefields of Europe, ending the turmoil of the Revolution, at least temporarily.

Restoration

Although the monarchy had been abolished in France, it was to be a case of "The king is dead, long live the king!" There was merely a short gap between the death of Louis XVI in 1793 and the next king to officially be accepted on the throne, his brother, who was crowned Louis XVIII in 1814. The monarch during this gap, Louis XVII, had only been recognized by a fervent group of monarchists and died from tuberculosis at the age of ten in 1795.

The gap before the restoration of the monarchy was largely filled by the arrival of Napoléon Bonaparte, who became Emperor Napoléon I in 1804. It was Napoléon who gave back France its pride as a nation. Today, he is remembered as one of the greatest Frenchmen of all time, and his grand tomb in the Dôme Church at Les Invalides is the most impressive burial place in the city.

If the arrival of the 19th century seemed to bring France a new regime and a new pride, it was also to bring the country—and Paris in particular—some of its finest literary talents. Stendhal, Honoré de Balzac, Victor Hugo, Alexandre Dumas *père*, Eugène Sue, and George Sand were all born between 1783 and 1804. Thus in a span of 21 years, no fewer than six distinguished canonical writers were born in France, and three names in particular, Stendhal, Balzac, and Hugo, were to dominate the period in which they were writing.

STENDHAL

Stendhal was born in the town of Grenoble in southeastern France, not far from the Italian border. His real name was Marie-Henri Beyle. His mother died when he was seven, and he never felt very close to his father. In 1799, at the tender age of 16, he left for Paris. His motivation for leaving was partly to sit for a college entrance examination at the École Polytechnique (Polytechnic School), and partly to escape his rather isolated provincial upbringing. He also wanted to try fulfilling his secret ambition of becoming a playwright.

A year after arriving in Paris, Beyle joined Napoléon Bonaparte's army. He only stayed in the army for a few years before he returned to Paris and entered into the Bohemian lifestyle suited to the would-be writer. Beyle was an enthusiastic writer, but by all accounts he lacked discipline since he began far more projects than he ever finished. He published nothing of note in these early years, although the diaries he kept at the time were published posthumously and make interesting reading. He attended drama classes and wanted to be the next Molière, who was a great literary hero to him. In the end, he would make his name as a novelist rather than a playwright.

By 1806, Beyle had run out of money, so he joined the army once more, this time staying until Napoléon fell from power in 1814. At that point, Beyle went to live in Italy because supporters of Napoléon were banned from France. Italy was a country Beyle had fallen in love with during his army career. In 1817 he published a two volume *History of Painting in Italy and Rome, Naples, and Florence*. Beyle, who used over 150 different pseudonyms over the course of his career, adopted "Stendhal" as his name for his *History*: the book's mild success led him to use the name more regularly.

In 1821, the ban on Napoléon's followers was lifted and Stendhal returned to Paris. This timing was convenient, because he was being thrown out of Italy for supporting an underground political movement. Back in Paris, Stendhal resumed the lifestyle of the writer, even if he was not as yet a successful one. He lounged in cafés, went to salons, kept diaries, and wrote constantly. He published *Racine and Shakespeare*, a sort of manifesto for romanticism, in 1821. The following year he published a semi-autobiographical book, *De l'amour* (*On Love*), which gained him some notoriety. In the salons he had a reputation as a wit and as a rather unconventional thinker, because some of his ideas on politics and romance were fairly advanced for their time.

During the late 1820s, Stendhal lived at 61 rue de Richelieu. This brought him even closer to his hero, for this was the same street on which Molière had lived—at number 40—and where his body had been taken after he died on stage in 1673. Stendhal's works began to be published more frequently, and they included a biography of the composer Gioacchino Rossini and a book about Stendhal's travels in Rome. It was also while living at 61 rue de Richelieu that Stendhal wrote the novel that became his literary masterpiece, *Le rouge et le noir* (*The Red and the Black*), which was published in 1830. It tells the story of the son of a carpenter who goes to Paris to escape his provincial upbringing, so it has autobiographical overtones, though it is also based on an account of the criminal career of Antoine Berthet, about which Stendhal had probably read in *La Gazette Tribuneaus*, a paper that carried news of the legal trials of the day.

THE SECOND RESTORATION

By the time *The Red and the Black* was published, the period known as the Second Restoration was in full swing. In December 1804, Napoléon had crowned himself Emperor in Notre-Dame Cathedral. Like a modern celebrity, Bonaparte kept the crowds—including the pope—waiting for hours. When the ceremony finally got underway, it was filled with the kind of over-the-top opulence that the French Revolution had tried to extinguish. During the ceremony, Pope Pius VII should have crowned Napoléon, but instead Napoléon took the crown from the pope and placed it on his own head, declaring himself emperor. It was not a good omen for a new kind of society.

Within less than a year, Napoléon had already suffered a major setback in his plans to expand the French Empire. He hoped to invade France's old enemy, England, but he was defeated by Lord Nelson in 1805 at the Battle of Trafalgar. Napoléon then strengthened the French Army and turned his attention to the east, defeating both the Austrian and Russian armies. His most notable victory was the Battle of Austerlitz, when Napoléon's army defeated a much larger coalition of Russian and Austrian troops. It was a victory commemorated by the creation of the Arc de Triomphe, and scenes from the battle can still be seen today in the friezes on the sides of the arch.

The triumphs were not to last, though. In 1808, Napoléon fought to gain control over Spain, a victory that was extremely costly. Napoléon's downward spiral continued in 1812, when he threw his all into a battle against the Russians. The vast Russian nation—and the harsh Russian winter—proved too much for Napoléon and his army, and he had to retreat in a humiliating defeat. By 1814, Napoléon was fighting to keep his own power in France. He lost this fight and abdicated the throne. Napoléon was then exiled to Elba, an island off the Italian coast.

The monarchy returned under Louis XVIII, who was crowned king in 1814. There was an interruption in Louis XVIII's rule, when Napoléon escaped from exile and returned to Paris. Supported by his old army comrades, Napoléon took control of the country again, but this only lasted for a short period known as the Hundred Days. In 1815, Napoléon experienced a defeat that was even worse than those he had experienced at Trafalgar and in Russia. This massive new defeat was the Battle of Waterloo, where Napoléon was again beaten by an Anglo-Prussian army whose English troops were led by the Duke of Wellington.

Napoléon abdicated again and this time was exiled to the South Atlantic island of Saint Helena, where he died in 1821. Louis XVIII returned to the throne in 1815, and upon his death in 1824 he was succeeded by his brother, Charles X. The monarchy was back, but it had learned something from the lessons of the past. It now ruled more moderately, no longer seeking to conquer the rest of Europe. This period was known as the Second Restoration.

These turbulent historical events provided the background for Stendhal's novel, *The Red and the Black*. The title is never fully explained, but is thought to refer to the red of the army and the black of the church, the two forces which pull the central character, Julien Sorel, in different directions. The book is notable not only for the picture it paints of this period in French history, but also for the psychological depth of the hero. He is both sensitive and ambitious, and the sympathies the reader feels for the sensitive side of his nature tend to be mitigated by his ruthless ambition, as well as his equally ruthless treatment of women. Sorel is eventually executed for a crime of passion, and it is only while imprisoned that he reflects on what is truly valuable in life.

The Paris of the novel, "this modern Babylon" as Sorel's friend the Abbé Pirard refers to the city, is a place where reputations, and the lives to which they are attached, are made and broken merely by right or wrong gestures and tones of voice. Though Julien bridles at the idea of submitting to such an environment, he understands that his ambitions require him to make his way in Parisian high society. The drawing-room culture to which the extreme decorousness of the Paris nobility gave rise is typified, in Stendhal's view, by an equally extreme ennui: "The smallest living idea seemed an outrage. Despite good tone, perfect manners, the desire to be agreeable, boredom was written upon every brow. The young men who came to pay their respects, afraid to speak of anything that might lead to their being suspected of thinking, afraid to reveal some forbidden reading, became silent after a few elegantly phrased sentences on Rossini and the weather" (38). Sorel's sense of his own superiority to the fops and fawners who populate aristocratic circles leads him to play the humble role Paris expects of him perfectly, while retaining the air of bravery and native nobility that allow him to win the hearts of the urbane Mathilde de la Mole as well as the provincial Madame de Renal.

Stendhal's other great novel, *La chartreuse de Parme* (*The Charterhouse of Parma*), was published in 1839. As the title suggests, this novel is set not in France but in Parma, Italy. It does, however, include scenes depicting the Battle of Waterloo and describing the regime of Napoléon Bonaparte. By this time Stendhal was living near Rome, where he had moved in the early 1830s. While on a visit to Paris in 1843, Stendhal died and was buried in the Montmartre Cemetery. Today a statue of Stendhal, crafted by the renowned French artist Auguste Rodin, stands in the Luxembourg Gardens near the St-Michel entrance.

HONORÉ DE BALZAC

An equal if not even greater realist novelist than Stendhal is Honoré de Balzac. He was born in 1799 in Tours, which is a town on the banks of the River Loire about 140 miles (225 km) southwest of Paris. His family moved to Paris in 1815, and Balzac spent two years at school and then an additional three years studying the law as a lawyer's clerk. He qualified to practice law, but by this time he had already begun to write plays. Although the plays were totally unsuccessful, Balzac knew that he wanted to be a writer and not a lawyer and he persuaded his family to support him in this endeavor.

Throughout the 1820s, Balzac struggled. He took various jobs, including publishing and printing, to help his finances. Despite his efforts, none of these ventures prospered. One of his unsuccessful print shops was located at 17 rue Visconti, which later became the home of the artist Eugène Delacroix in 1836. It can still be seen today, although it is a private building.

Balzac had been short of money all his life, and in 1828 he

almost went bankrupt. He had amassed vast debt that would plague him for years on end. To escape these ever-mounting debts, Balzac wrote furiously. As a result, he was amazingly prolific: he produced about 100 novels during his lifetime, as well as short stories, plays, and articles. During this decade of struggle, he published several of his books. Although they were unsuccessful, Balzac was learning the craft that would eventually make him one of the greatest writers of 19th-century Europe.

Balzac's first notable book was published in 1829 and was called *Le dernier Chouan* (*The Last Chouan*), which was later changed to *Les Chouans* (*The Chouans*). The Chouans were peasants from Brittany, and the novel tells of their involvement in an attempted royalist insurrection in 1799. In 1830, Balzac published *Scènes de la vie privée* (*Scenes from Private Life*), and this collection of several long stories gives an intimate portrait of domestic life at the time, and also intimate portraits of the young girls at the heart of the stories. Even in these early works Balzac's characteristic gift for delineating the characters of everyone—men and women, upper class and lower class, selfless and selfish—was becoming apparent.

As Balzac's life continued, it became clear that his money troubles were not all due to unfortunate business dealings. He had always wanted to be at the center of Parisian society, and with these first two reasonably successful books he spent far more money than he could afford. He wanted to dress well, attend parties and literary salons, live the high life. It was not just show, though. He was also one of France's hardest-working authors. Balzac was known for putting in long days, resulting in the large volume of work that he produced throughout his career. He was renowned for drinking endless cups of strong, black coffee to keep him going. When Balzac was writing, nothing else mattered.

In 1832, Balzac began to correspond with a Polish countess, Éveline Hanska, who had contacted him to tell him how much she admired his work. She was far from being the only woman to write to the increasingly famous author in this way; many women had responded to the sympathetic female characters he created and seemed to understand with such depth. A relationship soon developed between Balzac and Hanska. The countess daringly promised that she would marry Balzac when her elderly husband died.

When he had begun corresponding with the countess, Balzac was approaching the peak of his writing career. This was fortune for him, since he was still in debt and wanted to clear his financial burden to enable him to marry the countess. In 1833, Balzac had the idea of producing a series of novels in which the characters would recur. This was not totally new—after all, Rabelais had written the series of books featuring Gargantua and Pantagruel some 350 years earlier—but it would be the first time a serious collection of novels featured strong recurring characters who would develop throughout the sequence of novels. It would deal with all levels of French society and portray the major events in France from the Revolution until Balzac's own time.

It was a mammoth undertaking, and it was not until 1840 that Balzac came up with a suitable title for the series: *La comédie humaine* (*The Human Comedy*). In 1842, he wrote the introduction to what he envisioned as no fewer than 150 interconnecting works of fiction, some of which were among the novels he had already published. He ended up writing some 90 of the books before his death. This was a phenomenal enterprise that can scarcely be imagined today, especially because his oeuvre included such classic stories as *Le père Goriot* (*Father Goriot*) and *La cousine Bette* (*Cousin Bette*), among many others. During this time, the husband of Éveline Hanska died. For various reasons, however, Hanska and Balzac still did not marry.

In 1840, the same year he had created the title for his upcoming series, Balzac moved into the house at 47 rue Raynouard. He lived there for the next seven years and today this address houses the Balzac Museum, more properly known as the Maison de Balzac (House of Balzac). He bought the house and lived in it using the name of Monsieur de Brugnol, because even though he was becoming well known and successful, he was still in debt and needed to hide from his creditors. For this reason, Balzac deliberately chose a house that also had a back door, leading into rue Berton, through which he could slip away if his creditors came to call. It is worth walking along this street today, because it has changed little and gives a glimpse of what Paris looked like during Balzac's time.

It was at this address that Balzac wrote most of his finest works, sitting at the desk that is on display there today. The house also contains many of the author's original manuscripts, his desk, memorabilia, a room devoted to the many film and stage adaptations of his works, and a special room dedicated to Éveline Hanska. By the time Balzac moved out of the house in 1847, the two were still not married and would not do so until March 1850. Balzac died only five months later. He is buried in the cemetery at Père-Lachaise in eastern Paris.

VICTOR HUGO

Balzac was certainly not the only great writer to grace the city of Paris during this time. One of his contemporaries was the much-respected author Victor Hugo. Hugo was born in 1802 in Besançon, a town almost 250 miles (402 km) to the southeast of Paris and only about 30 miles (48 km) from Switzerland. His father was a general and the family moved around a little, with Hugo being educated partly in Madrid and partly in Paris at the École Polytechnique.

Hugo was a talented child and he decided from an early age that he wanted to be a writer. By the age of 14, he had written his first play. At 15, he won a poetry award from l'Académie française, and by the age of 20 he had published his first book, a collection of poems called *Odes et poésies diverses*. He soon began publishing his works regularly, including more books of verse, as well as novels and dramas. Most of these are now almost forgotten, overshadowed as they were by his later and more memorable works. However, a preface he wrote to a play about the life of Oliver Cromwell, the 17th-century English politician, is now seen as the manifesto for what became the romantic movement, a cry to leave behind the stricter rules of classical writing.

The first of Hugo's great works was published in 1831 as *Notre-Dame de Paris*, which means "Our Lady of Paris." The book was named after the city's great cathedral. When it was later translated into English, however, the title was changed to *The Hunchback of Notre-Dame* in order to emphasize the main character. The book is set in the 15th century and tells the story of the hunchback, Quasimodo, who lives in the towers up among the gargoyles of the cathedral. The gothic building is so grand in scale that it is still possible to visit it today, look up, and think that Quasimodo might still be up in the rafters somewhere.

Construction on this landmark began in 1163, and it took large teams of master craftsmen and laborers 170 years of work before it was completed. The cathedral was almost destroyed during the Revolution, linked as it was with the crowning of kings and queens through the centuries. Even for Napoléon's crowning after the Revolution in 1804, the cathedral was crumbling and parts of it had to be hidden behind wall hangings and tapestries. It had even been sold at one point to a scrap dealer, but it had never actually been demolished.

When Hugo's book was published in 1831, the cathedral was still decaying slowly. He was determined to do something about what was, after all, the spiritual heart not only of Paris, but also of all France. Hugo mounted a campaign to raise funds and to restore the building to its former glory. People rallied around the project, and work began in 1841. After 23 years of work, the cathedral was restored to the splendor still seen today.

By this time Hugo had become successful, and in 1833 he had acquired a rather grand house on a corner of the place des Vosges, at number 6. He lived there for the next 15 years, and it remains today as the Maison Victor Hugo (Victor Hugo Museum). Inside are manuscripts, photographs, furniture, and sculptures. The museum also contains photographs both of and by Hugo, who was extremely interested in the new invention of photography.

While living at the place des Vosges, Hugo produced a large number of books. He became an honored member of Parisian society and was elected to the prestigious l'Académie française in 1841. Hugo became increasingly interested in politics during this time, but he seemed to go from one extreme to another. His family members were staunch supporters of Napoléon Bonaparte, but in his youth Hugo had become a supporter of the monarchy. He was honored by King Louis-Philippe in 1845, but by 1848 Hugo had become a Republican. He was vehemently against the 1848 coup d'état by Napoléon III. As a result, Hugo was exiled by the new emperor and lived on the island of Guernsey in the Channel Islands from 1851 to 1870.

The exile did not diminish Hugo's literary powers in any way. In fact, in 1862 he produced what is considered his greatest work, *Les misérables*, which usually retains its French title in English translations because the meaning is so evidently clear. This novel deals with the underside of Parisian society in the 19th century. *Les misérables* includes descriptions of an area called the Cour des Miracles (Courtyard of Miracles). This name referred to the miracles that occurred there every night when the blind and lame beggars could see and walk again when they returned home after the day's begging was done. The Cour des Miracles was situated close to Les Halles, which at that time was a huge marketplace. The beggars would build themselves shelters made out of wooden boards taken from the market. The area was effectively what today might be called a shantytown, and it was eventually flattened by the city authorities.

In 1870, Hugo returned to France after the Second Empire had collapsed. He became more left wing in his views, while at the same time being elected to the French equivalent of the senate in 1876. When he died in 1885, he was so revered that his body lay in state underneath the Arc de Triomphe, but was taken at his request in a pauper's hearse to its final resting place at the Panthéon, where his tomb can still be seen today.

DUMAS *PÈRE* AND DUMAS *FILS*

If *The Hunchback of Notre-Dame* created a romantic fiction around Notre-Dame Cathedral, then *The Man in the Iron Mask* did the same for the Bastille. Although the existence of the mysterious man was a fact, the novel written by Alexandre Dumas was fiction. Dumas based the story on a rumor apparently created by Voltaire, which suggested that the man was in reality the brother of King Louis XIV, a story with little evidence to back it up. It did, however, make for a good novel.

Dumas wrote several swashbuckling novels that have stood the test of time, and his creations have lived on both in print and on film, right through into the 21st century. The two most famous of his works are *The Count of Monte Cristo* and *The Three Musketeers*, which successfully wove fact with fiction. Dumas was renowned in his day for being cavalier with the truth, and he was known to borrow stories, even from other writers, and turn them into good romantic reads. *The Adventures of a Younger Son*, for example, was written by the English author Edward John Trelawney, and yet Dumas claimed the French version as one of his own works.

Dumas had been born about 50 miles (80 km) from Paris in the Picardy region in 1802, and he came to the city in 1823. He first wrote plays, which were very successful at the time though they are not so well known today. He followed these plays with a series of novels, some written in collaboration with other authors and some inspired by other sources. He undoubtedly worked extremely hard and is said to have produced more than 1,000 full-length works, which made him very wealthy indeed. His two greatest successes both came in 1844, which ought to provide some indication of his prodigious output. He lived most of his life in Paris, when he wasn't traveling throughout Europe, and was buried in his hometown of Villers-Cotterêts when he died in 1870.

In 1824, another person by the name of Alexandre Dumas was born in Paris. He was the illegitimate son of the famous author by one of his many mistresses. Like his father, the young

Dumas became a writer. Since the father and son shared the same name and both worked as writers, they are usually distinguished by being called Dumas *père* (father) and Dumas *fils* (son), or the elder and the younger, or senior and junior. Dumas *père* was said to have complained that if he had known his son was going to follow in his footsteps, he would have given him another name.

Dumas *fils* was successful, although never to the extent that his father had been, and today he is mainly remembered for one of his plays, *Camille*. This was an adaptation of his first novel, published in 1848 as *La dame aux camélias* (*The Lady of the Camelias*). It has been performed countless times with many famous actresses attracted to the role of the courtesan, based on a real-life character, who is kept in her place by the hypocrisy of

Hugo's Home

The place des Vosges has not always been a prestigious address. It was first laid out in 1612 when it was known as the Royal Square. King Henri IV was the person responsible for turning the Marais into a fashionable district, with the Royal Square at its heart. The perfectly symmetrical square—with 36 arcaded buildings overlooking a central open area, where today children play and lovers stroll—was the most beautiful in the city. In 1800, it was renamed the place des Vosges, after the Vosges district of northeastern France, but it had already begun to decline ever since the royal court had moved from Paris to the new palace at Versailles.

When Victor Hugo moved to this area in 1833, the square was still beautiful. It was far from being as fashionable and expensive as it is today, however. Its resurgence only began when André Malraux, Paris's culture minister in the 1960s, designated the whole of the Marais an area of historical importance that was to be renovated and preserved.

the ostensibly respectable society. The play was also the basis of
the opera *La Traviata*, by the Italian composer Giuseppe Verdi.
Dumas *fils* died in 1895, and his grave can be found in the
cemetery at Montmartre.

GEORGE SAND

The romantic movement in Paris was certainly male-dominated, but there is one female writer who made her mark, if not
quite to the same extent as Victor Hugo, or Balzac. She was
born in 1804, and her real name was Amandine-Aurore-Lucie
Dupin, the Baronne Dudevant. She is now known by the pseudonym she adopted: George Sand.

The need to adopt a male pen name shows how hard it was at
that time for a woman to be accepted as a writer. A female contemporary of hers in England was writing under the name
George Eliot, for similar reasons. French society considered
writing novels no job for a woman. George Sand was no conventional woman, however. Though she had been born in Paris,
she spent most of her early life outside the city. She returned at
the age of 27, bringing her two children and escaping from an
unhappy marriage.

George Sand scandalized respectable Parisian society with her
unconventional views and her love affairs. It was accepted that
men would have mistresses, but for a woman to have a lover was
considered quite shocking. Her first lover was a writer, Jules
Sandeau. The couple worked together, publishing two novels
under the name of Jules Sand. In 1832, she published her own
first novel, *Indiana*, under the name George Sand. She went on
to write many more novels and she was certainly as prolific as
her male contemporaries. She has always been more famous for
her life and loves than for her literary works, however.

Sand was part of a group of artists known as the Romantics,
which included painters such as Jean-Auguste-Dominique
Ingres and Eugène Delacroix. The group also included musicians such as Franz Liszt and Frédéric Chopin, who became
Sand's lover in 1837. The group often met at the home of a

Dutch artist named Ary Scheffer. Scheffer lived at 16 rue Chaptal, which now houses the Musée de la Vie Romantique (Museum of Romantic Life). It is a small, charming museum that contains paintings, furniture, jewelry, manuscripts, and other mementoes of that period.

Sand died in 1876, and few of her novels have remained in print. Interest in her life has remained constant, increasingly so in recent years because she has become regarded as an early feminist and a strong woman unfairly overlooked in a male-dominated society. Her autobiography, *Histoire de ma vie* (*The Story of My Life*), evokes this period in Parisian history when literature was finally blooming.

CHAPTER SIX

The Second Empire

The first half of the 19th century had dealt with the aftermath of the Revolution and a government in a constant state of instability. As the latter half of the 19th century dawned, however, the people of France looked forward to a new era. It was a time when France and several other developed nations in western Europe were heading into the Industrial Revolution. During this time, France's economy prospered, poverty was not as widespread as it had been earlier, and the arts flourished.

This was also time Paris started to become more recognizable as the city it is today. Streetlamps began to illuminate Parisian nights beginning in 1757, and proper sidewalks began to appear in 1782. Beginning in 1850, the city had new water supply and sewage systems. As the face of the city took on a new character, so did its government.

In 1830, there had been another revolution. It seemed that France's monarchs had not learned from the lessons of history after all, and so they were condemned to repeat their mistakes. In 1829, King Charles X had appointed a ministry that was filled with his most fervent pro-Royalist supporters. The Chamber of Deputies voted to reject these appointments in

March 1830. The king then dissolved the chamber and held new elections. The result was the same, so the king decided to ignore it. He again called for new elections, which he had rigged. He also censored members of the press so that they could not report freely on what was taking place. Journalists said this was a flagrant breach of the constitution, and the people of Paris rallied to their cause. Several days of rioting took place in the streets, and the king's army was driven out of the city.

Since he had such little support, King Charles X abdicated and Louis-Philippe, the Duke of Orléans, ascended to the throne. At the same time, the king's powers were reduced to ensure that these problems would not happen again. By the late 1840s, however, the monarchy was dealt another blow. The country was suffering a depression and many people blamed the monarchy, saying life had been better under the Republic. The Republican movement gained strength, and in February 1848 its followers held a rally. Government troops tried to quell the rally, which resulted in violence. The situation quickly worsened, turning into the kind of full-fledged revolution that Paris had seen in the previous century. Before February was over, King Louis-Philippe had abdicated and an ad hoc republican government had been established to rule in his place.

France was now under the Second Republic, but the transition was far from smooth. There was a vicious struggle between moderate Republicans and radical Republicans, and the streets of Paris still ran red with blood as the factions struggled for power. In 1851 Louis-Napoléon, a nephew of Napoléon Bonaparte, stepped in and took advantage of the turmoil to seize power for himself. He became Napoléon III.

At first, Napoléon III ruled France quite strictly. Gradually, however, he allowed a more modern kind of parliamentary democracy to emerge, albeit one with the emperor still in charge. Napoléon III could afford to be more liberal, because depressions were becoming a thing of the past in the newly expanding industrial economy. The arrival of the railways increased trade and allowed people to travel, and Paris itself was about to be transformed magnificently.

The architect of the transformation was Baron Georges-Eugène Haussmann. Haussmann was in charge of public works under Napoléon III from 1852 to 1870, virtually the whole duration of the Second Republic. Haussmann developed Paris's railway stations, sewers, water supply, streetlights, and domestic gas supplies. He also built several parks, including the vast Bois de Boulogne in the west and Bois de Vincennes in the east.

Haussmann's changes transformed Paris into a modern, beautiful city, and it remains so even now. For that reason, Haussmann is revered today. During his own time, however, he was reviled. Haussmann's vision of wide, tree-lined boulevards was achieved at the expense of the densely packed population that existed at the time. He swept away thousands of houses, and tens of thousands of people were forced out of the city center. When Haussmann began working on the Île de la Cité, for example, its population was 25,000. When he finished, the island's population had been reduced to just 1,000 people. These changes were not purely aesthetic, however. It was part of Napoléon III's plan to make the streets easier for his army to negotiate. While at the same time, he wanted to make it harder for any rebelling citizens to erect barricades across the streets, as had happened in the earlier revolutions.

CHARLES PIERRE BAUDELAIRE

As Haussmann's work was giving Paris a new and more modern look, writers were also surveying the city from original perspectives. The first author of any note during this period was Baudelaire. Charles-Pierre Baudelaire was born in Paris in 1821 and was only six years old when his father, a civil servant who had a talent for painting and poetry, died. The young Baudelaire then lived alone with his mother, and he cherished this time they shared together because he was very close to her. This idyllic time was interrupted, however, when his mother remarried. Baudelaire detested his new stepfather, and evidently the feeling was mutual.

Baudelaire was a talented student who began writing poetry early, and he knew from a young age that he wanted to be a writer. This was an ambition of which his mother and stepfather disapproved, however. As a result, Baudelaire began to study law, but he spent much of his time reveling in the lowlife on the Left Bank. Before he was 20 years old, Baudelaire had already contracted a sexually transmitted disease from a prostitute. This disease would eventually kill him.

Baudelaire's parents were so concerned about both his career choice and the lifestyle he was leading that they sent him on a long sea journey to India in 1841. They hoped this would break the ties to the unsavory aspects of his lifestyle. The young man demanded to be let off the ship, however. On the Indian Ocean's island of Mauritius, Baudelaire left the ship and returned to Paris. He was more determined than ever to become a writer, as well as resume his dissolute lifestyle.

In 1842, Baudelaire turned 21. Since he was legally an adult he was able to inherit the money left to him by his real father. In 1847, he began reading the works of American author Edgar Allan Poe, to whom he felt such a spiritual kinship that he came to regard him almost as a second self. Before long, Baudelaire became known for his French translations of Poe's work. These translations were so well received in part because Baudelaire enjoyed and identified with Poe's writing so much, but also because Poe, unlike many other great writers, tends to benefit by translation. Baudelaire went on to do several more translations over the next few years.

Money flowed into Baudelaire's pockets, but it just as quickly flowed out again due to his extravagant lifestyle. He bought an apartment in the Hôtel de Lauzun at 17 quai d'Anjou on the Île St-Louis, where he organized meetings of his Hashish Club. The hotel still exists today, although it is rather more respectable after it was restored in 1928 for use by visiting heads of state. Baudelaire was also a visitor at number 9 quai d'Anjou, just down the street. It was the home of his friend Honoré Daumier, who was a painter and notorious caricaturist. It was also the place where Baudelaire met the artist Eugène Delacroix.

Baudelaire shocked Parisian society by taking a West Indian mistress named Jeanne Duval. She was known as the Black Venus and lived on the Île St-Louis at 6 rue le Regrattier, a house that still exists as a private residence today. If their relationship shocked society, then it was to be shocked even more when Baudelaire produced the collection of poems for which he is most remembered, *Les fleurs du mal* (*The Flowers of Evil*). Baudelaire had written the poems when he was living in a hotel at 19 quai Voltaire, which still has rooms for rent today.

Les fleurs du mal came out in book form in 1857, although it had originally been published in a magazine two years earlier. The phrase *flowers of evil* refers to the temptations of the flesh, which Baudelaire felt powerless to resist and which eventually led to his death. The book was written in six sections, and it partially chronicles one man's journey through life. Because the man was Baudelaire, the poems dealt with his journey in what was, for the time, explicit detail, including his relationships with various mistresses.

One section, called "Tableaux parisiens" ("Parisian Scenes"), describes a day in the life of the city through the eyes of the narrator. Baudelaire championed quotidian reality over transcendent conceptions of beauty, and this inclination inspired in turn, as it was to do for the modernists of the 20th century, a greater sympathy for the urban than for the pastoral as a setting proper to poetic vision. Before "Parisian Scenes," not much lyrical poetry had been devoted to cities: Verlaine, Rimbaud, Crane, Eliot, Sandburg, and others may be said to have followed a route Baudelaire discovered for poetry in adding the group of poems to *Les fleurs du mal*. The Paris presented in "Parisian Scenes" shares in the pathos and irony that characterizes Baudelaire's verse elsewhere: "The heat and hiss of kitchens can be felt here and there,/The panting of heavy bands, the theatres' clamour./Cheap hotels, the haunts of dubious solaces,/Are filling with tarts, and crooks, their sleek accomplices,/And thieves, who have never heard of restraint or remorse/Return now to their work as a matter of course/Forcing safes behind carefully re-locked doors,/To get a few days' living and put clothes on their whores." The poem, ironically titled "Comes the Charming Evening," ends by asking pity for the less fortunate: "Indeed, many a one has never even known/The hearth's warm charm. Pity such a one" (99). In another poem from the "Scenes" group, the sun shining into the labyrinthine city streets is likened to the function of the poet: "When [the sun] comes

The Final Address

Paris has several fascinating cemeteries, but the most famous of them all is Père-Lachaise, which is northeast of the city center. It might seem morbid to spend time in a cemetery, but Père-Lachaise is a fascinating place. It is the largest cemetery in the city, at about 100 acres (40 ha) in size, and with 3,000 trees and countless statues, it is a pleasant place to stroll and it is easy to spend half a day here.

One of the fascinations with this cemetery, of course, is the number of famous people who are buried there. This is the final resting place of many literary figures, including Gérard de Nerval, Marcel Proust, Molière, Oscar Wilde, Honoré de Balzac, Sidonie-Gabrielle Colette, Guillaume Apollinaire, Gertrude Stein, and Richard Wright. There are many other notable names whose graves are also worth seeking out and these include the composers Gioacchino Rossini and Frédéric Chopin, the artists Eugène Delacroix, Amedeo Modigliani, and Camille Corot, the actress Sarah Bernhardt, the dancer Isadora Duncan, the politician Adolphe Thiers, the singer Edith Piaf, and perhaps the most notorious of all, the rock singer Jim Morrison. Morrison's grave is always quite a sight, adorned as it is with messages and flowers, and usually a few fans too.

down into the city like a poet/Transfiguring the values of things the most abject,/He enters like royalty, unaccompanied by officials,/All the palatial hotels and all the hospitals" (79). Paris put Baudelaire in touch with the extremes of society—those luxuriating in its hotels and those seeking help in its hospitals—and offered them to him as they are offered to the sun and to "royalty," freely, under natural conditions, without the meddling of "officials."

Paris's "officials" kept an eye on Baudelaire's book though: *Les fleurs du mal* was so shocking that legal action was taken against 13 of the poems, on the grounds of offending public decency or mocking religion. Baudelaire went to court in August 1857. He was fined, and six of the poems had to be removed from the book on the grounds of obscenity. Despite their notoriety, the poems were unsuccessful. This caused Baudelaire to despair; he had put his life and his art into the poems. He revised them and published a new edition in 1861. That same year he tried, without success, to get himself elected to l'Académie française. It was unlikely that this respectable body would elect someone with Baudelaire's bawdy reputation.

Baudelaire's situation worsened as time passed. The publisher of his new version of *Les fleurs du mal* went bankrupt. Then in 1864, Baudelaire went to live in Brussels in the hope of finding a Belgian publisher for the work. While there, Baudelaire's health deteriorated. In 1866, he collapsed in the street and was stricken with paralysis. He returned to Paris, only to spend the last year of his life in a nursing home. Baudelaire died in 1867 and was buried in the cemetery of Montparnasse. At the time of his death, most of Baudelaire's work was either unpublished or out of print. It was only after his death that later poets, including Paul Verlaine and T.S. Eliot, recognized Baudelaire's talent. Today, a statue in his honor now stands in the Luxembourg Gardens.

GÉRARD DE NERVAL

Baudelaire was the first major writer of what became known as the symbolist movement. It began in Paris in the latter half of the 19th century. The movement encouraged writers to express their thoughts and feelings through the use of unusually private symbols rather than explicit statements. It also encouraged writers to throw out the rigid structures of verse forms and to use their imaginations much more freely. One writer whose was using these techniques before the symbolist movement even began is Gérard de Nerval.

Nerval, whose real name was Gérard Labrunie, was born in Paris in 1808. His father was a doctor with Napoléon's army, and he was stationed in Germany. The young child and his mother remained in France. When Nerval was two years old, his mother died and he was sent to live with relatives in the country. This idyllic rural upbringing is something he harked back to in his writing, as his own later life was much more tempestuous.

When he was twelve, Nerval returned to Paris to live with his father. By the age of 20, he had written a highly praised translation of *Faust*, a play by the renowned German writer Johann Wolfgang von Goethe. In 1836, Nerval met an actress named Jenny Colon and fell madly in love with her. Two years later, she married another man and Nerval was devastated. Colon died four years later, and Nerval was heartbroken. He sought solace in travel overseas and in his writing, which dealt with fantasies and dream images.

Increasingly, Nerval became mentally disturbed and was admitted to institutions several times. Despite this, he continued to produce writings that would later be described as surrealist and symbolist, although his work predated both those movements. Nerval's mental anguish continued, and in 1855 his body was found hanging from a lamppost in rue de la Vieille Lanterne. He is buried in the cemetery of Père-Lachaise.

GUSTAVE FLAUBERT

There could hardly be a greater contrast with the life of Nerval than that of Gustave Flaubert, who became one of the preeminent French authors of the time. His book, *L'Education senti-*

mentale (*Sentimental Education*), is mentioned in Woody Allen's film *Annie Hall*, when Allen's character lists what he regards as life's greatest pleasures. In complete contrast to Nerval's approach to writing, Flaubert became known as the greatest master of the realist school of French literature.

Flaubert was born in Rouen, Normandy, in 1821. He began writing as a young boy, and by the time he was 16 he had completed an unpublished novel that told of his passionate love for a much older woman. By the time he came to Paris at the age of 20 to study law, Flaubert was already a published author. He was soon able to devote his life totally to writing, although not in the way he would necessarily have chosen. When he was 22, Flaubert's studies had to cease because he was diagnosed as suffering from a kind of nervous disorder, possibly a type of epilepsy. His father died soon afterward, and so too did his sister. This left Flaubert to spend most of the rest of his life with his mother, near Rouen.

He did visit Paris regularly, though, and on one visit in 1846 met a poet named Louise Colet, who was to be his mistress for eight years. Although he was constantly writing, much of this work did not appear until he had become firmly established with his first and greatest novel, *Madame Bovary*.

Madame Bovary was published in 1857 and is considered a landmark in French literature. Though not set in Paris, it is a book that cannot be ignored. Emma Bovary has a dull provincial life and marriage, but yearns for the kind of exciting life she reads about. She embarks on a series of affairs, which she initially sees as grand passions, but ultimately she realizes that her life has not changed, and finally she commits suicide. The novel was hailed as a remarkably intimate story, and great surprise was expressed at how a man could get so convincingly into the mind of a woman. Flaubert's answer was simple: "*Madame Bovary, c'est moi*" ("Madame Bovary is me").

The book had taken Flaubert five years to write and when first published it was considered immoral. For this reason, the author was taken to court in Paris, although he was acquitted of the charge. This was only six months before the poet Baudelaire would face similar charges and be found guilty.

Flaubert's status as the leading writer of the day was confirmed when his highly regarded historical novel *Salammbô*, set in ancient Carthage, was published in 1863. Then in 1870, *Sentimental Education* was published. This *bildungsroman*, now regarded as a classic, was not highly praised at the time. As well as offering yet another sympathetic portrait of its characters, *Sentimental Education* was set during the events that led to the coup d'état by Louis Napoléon in 1851, and provides a great understanding of French life at that time.

The last few years of Flaubert's life were not happy. He had financial problems, and two plays that he wrote were both failures. In 1880, he died suddenly of a stroke while sitting at his kitchen table working on his final, unfinished novel, *Bouvard and Pécuchet*. Although Flaubert died at his home near Rouen, a statue in his memory stands in the Luxembourg Gardens in Paris. Before his death, Flaubert's major pleasure had been the friendships he had formed with a new generation of writers, including his close friend Guy de Maupassant, and the towering figure of Émile Zola, who was waiting in the wings.

CHAPTER SEVEN

The Third Republic and
the Dawn of the 20th Century

During Napoléon III's reign, he had succeeded in establishing strong French ties with Germany. At this time, northern Germany and northern Poland were part of a large state called Prussia. Prussia's prime minister, Otto von Bismarck, wanted to sever the strong ties France and Germany had created. In July 1870, the Franco-Prussian War broke out and quickly grew into a disaster for France. By that autumn, Paris was under siege. There were food shortages and some citizens were killing dogs, cats, and any other animals they could catch in order to survive.

In January 1871, Paris was forced to surrender. A new French government was put in place and a politician named Adolphe Thiers was chosen to be the first president of the Third Republic. By March, various groups of citizens in Paris were rebelling against this new government and formed what they regarded as their own revolutionary government, which was known as the Paris Commune. Among their complaints was that many of the members of the new government were ardent royalists in favor of restoring the monarchy yet again. Members of the Paris Commune also argued against the terms of the surrender to the Prussians. They regarded the terms as humiliating to France and were in favor of resuming hostilities. The Paris Commune was short-lived, and government troops broke it up in March 1871.

After the Paris Commune had been dismantled, the terms of surrender were implemented. France was forced to surrender parts of its eastern territories of Alsace and Lorraine to the Germans, and pay incredibly heavy war reparation of 5 billion gold francs. The money was paid by the fall of 1873, at which point the final troops withdrew from French territory.

If this short-lived war was to be humiliating for France politically, and devastating financially, it certainly had no ill effect on the French artistic scene in the final years of the 19th century and the start of the 20th century. It was the period that gave rise to the Eiffel Tower, the Paris métro system, the invention of cinematography by the Lumière brothers, and the popular artistic movement known as impressionism. It was also the period when numerous distinguished French writers rose to prominence. They included Émile Zola, Guy de Maupassant, Stéphane Mallarmé, Anatole France, Paul Verlaine, Arthur Rimbaud, Georges Feydeau, André Gide, Guillaume Apollinaire, Sidonie-Gabrielle Colette, and the great Parisian chronicler, Marcel Proust. It was also a period when some of the first important foreign writers—including Henry James and Oscar Wilde—moved to Paris, setting a trend that would continue throughout the 20th century.

GUY DE MAUPASSANT

One of the most well-known writers of this period was Guy de Maupassant. Today, his short stories are still considered to be among the finest examples of the genre ever written. Maupassant was born near the Normandy port of Dieppe, on the northern coast of France, in 1850. It was less than 40 miles (64 km) from Gustave Flaubert's home near Rouen, and the two families were friendly.

The young Maupassant was one of a group of writers who sat at the feet of the great Flaubert, whose work undoubtedly influenced the youth. Maupassant's mother had been a childhood friend of Flaubert, and she had written to the distinguished author asking him to do what he could to help her own son's writing career. Flaubert was happy to oblige, but there can be no doubt that the young Maupassant would have succeeded anyway through his own talents.

Maupassant went to Paris in 1869 to study law, as did many writers before him. He then volunteered to serve in the army during the Franco-Prussian War, and many of his later stories would be based on his these experiences. After serving in that ill-fated war, Maupassant returned to his law studies in Paris. He was not keen to practice law and instead embarked on a career as a civil servant. He was not altogether happy in this pursuit either, but he was successful and gained seniority in his various positions.

During this time, the would-be author was still meeting with his mother's friend Flaubert, and the two would often dine together when Flaubert visited Paris. The Café de la Paix at 3 place de l'Opéra was one of Maupassant's favorite spots, as indeed it was for other writers and artists including Émile Zola, André Gide, Oscar Wilde, and Salvador Dalí. The Lapérouse restaurant overlooking the Seine at 51 quai des Grands-Augustins was another favorite spot for Maupassant, who loved the river and the sea, both of which he featured in his fiction. At these meetings, Flaubert would read what his protégé had written and comment on it, all the while encouraging the writer who he believed to be talented.

Despite Flaubert's guidance, Maupassant had only managed to publish a handful of stories, most of them in small and unknown publications. Then in 1880, Maupassant's career reached a turning point. That April, he had his first major success when his story "Boule de suif" ("Ball of Fat") was included in a collection of six stories by leading authors of the day, including Émile Zola. Maupassant's contribution was regarded as eclipsing even Zola's, and his name was made. Today, "Boule de suif" is still regarded today as one of the finest stories Maupassant ever produced.

The success of that one story brought Maupassant invitations from newspaper and magazine editors to contribute his stories to their publications. These invitations allowed Maupassant to leave his job and concentrate on writing. He went on to publish more than 300 stories, not to mention several novels and non-fiction books. His best novel is considered to be *Bel-Ami* (*Good Friend*), which appeared in 1885. It reveals the ruthless ambition and the cynicism at the heart of the Parisian society, with which he had become familiar.

The last decade of Maupassant's life was one of constant work and constant success. He earned enough money to acquire several homes and yachts, as well as his apartment in Paris. Despite this material success, a sexually transmitted disease Maupassant had contracted as a young man caught up with him. This, along with the death of his brother in an asylum, drove Maupassant to despair. He tried to kill himself in 1892, and his mother had

Maupassant's View

Guy de Maupassant said that he liked dining at the Eiffel Tower, because then he didn't have to look at it. What is now known and loved worldwide as the symbol of Paris was not universally popular when it first appeared. Many writers and artists—including Maupassant, Émile Zola, Paul Verlaine, and Alexandre Dumas *fils*—signed the Petition of the 300, protesting the tower's appearance on the banks of the Seine.

When built for the 1889 Universal Exhibition, the tower was never intended to be permanent but the structure's general popularity ensured that it remained intact. At 1,050 feet (320 km) high, it was then the tallest building in the world, and remained so until New York's Empire State Building was constructed in 1931. Today, despite what Maupassant said, it is a delight to sit anywhere in the city and dine with a view of the Eiffel Tower.

him committed to an asylum. He was later removed to a nursing home in Paris, where he died in 1893. His grave, displaying an open book, is in the cemetery at Montparnasse.

ÉMILE ZOLA

If Maupassant was the master of the short story, then the master of the novel during the final decades of the 19th century was Émile Zola. He is, in fact, considered to be one of the greatest French novelists of any century, and he took the novel to new heights—some might say depths—of realism. His sequence of 20 connected novels that fell under the collective title of *Les Rougon-Macquart* was a triumph of literary imagination. The books told the story of French life at that time, across all levels of society, in a way that had never been done before—not even by Balzac with his even more ambitious *La comédie humaine.* Paris is at the center of many of those novels, giving as vivid a portrait of the city at that time as can be seen anywhere.

Zola had been born in Paris in 1840, although he spent much of his early life in Aix-en-Provence, where his father worked as a civil engineer. Zola went to school with Paul Cézanne, who would go on to achieve great fame as an artist. Cézanne and Zola remained friends for many years, and Zola wrote about the impressionist school of art in his fiction, where some of the artists of the day appear there in disguised form. In Paris, Cézanne introduced Zola to Édouard Manet, often called the father of impressionism, and Zola mingled with many of the artists in their favorite haunts in Montmartre. One of these was the Auberge (Inn) de la Bonne-Franquette on rue Norvins. It was a favorite spot of Cézanne, as well as other artists such as Claude Monet, Auguste Renoir, Henri Toulouse-Lautrec, and Vincent van Gogh among others. At that time, however, that distinguished collection of artists was not considered to be quite so distinguished.

Like many of the artists he kept company with, Zola had grown up in poverty. By the age of 25, he was able to support himself by his pen, producing stories, articles, poetry, criticism, and one novel that gained him some attention. It was to be the next novel, which he wrote at age 27, that would establish Zola as a writer to be reckoned with. *Thérèse Raquin* told a simple but violent tale of adultery and murder, carried out behind the scenes at a small shop in a Paris backstreet. Zola advocated naturalism in writing, and he practiced what he preached. The minutely observed details in his work create a convincing portrait of life in Paris, as well as other French cities and towns, at that time.

Among the most powerful of his many works are Zola's novels, many of which are still read today. One of these novels is *L'Assommoir* (*The Drunkard*), which tells of life in the Parisian slums. It is set in a world of absinthe bars in a district with the unofficial name of La Goutte-d'Or (The Drop of Gold), from the ancient vineyard that once existed there. It's an area behind the Gare du Nord station, north of the boulevard de la Chapelle. Another of Zola's novels is *Nana*, which depicts the story of a high-society prostitute named Nana, who grew up on rue de la Goutte-d'Or itself. Zola's novels also include *Germinal*, which tells the tale of a miners' strike, and *La débâcle* (*The Downfall*), which paints as convincing a picture of the downfall of France's Second Empire as any history book.

In 1886, Zola published *L'Oeuvre* (*The Masterpiece*), which told of the life of an artist similar to some of the impressionist friends he had made in Montmartre. Unfortunately the ending, in which the painter kills himself from frustration at being unable to express his vision in his work, was considered offensive by many of the real artists. Cézanne, in particular, took it as an attack upon himself. Despite the fact that Zola had staunchly defended the much-criticized impressionist movement in numerous newspaper articles, their close friendship ended.

Zola was seldom far from controversy, and no incident was more controversial than what became known as the Dreyfus Affair. In 1894, a Jewish officer who worked in the French Army, was convicted of treason. This officer's name was Alfred Dreyfus. Zola, like many others, realized early on that the man was innocent and that it was probably a case of anti-Semitism from the army authorities. The case divided French society, and in 1898 when the controversy was still raging, Zola used his prominent public position to defend the man. He published an open letter addressed to the French officials in the Parisian newspaper *L'Aurore*. Zola's letter began with words that have gone down in history and been repeated by others on similar occasions: *J'accuse* ("I accuse"). Zola accused the authorities of wrongful conviction and, worse, of deliberately concealing the truth.

Zola, in his turn, was charged with libel and found guilty. Zola was sentenced to imprisonment, but he appealed his case. In 1899, when it appeared that the appeal would be denied, Zola fled in exile to England. The next year, the Dreyfus case was reopened, and Zola returned to Paris to see Dreyfus cleared of the charges. Zola was praised for his principled stand against anti-Semitism and abuse of power, though others mocked him for fleeing the country instead of remaining to fight. In any event, his public accusation of the authorities, which proved to be justified, was seen as a significant act in the modern history of France.

Zola, who had so vehemently defended Dreyfus, died in 1902 at his home in Paris after being poisoned by fumes from a blocked chimney. It was seen as an accident, but there were those who did not discount the possibility that the chimney had been deliberately blocked either by the authorities or by fervent anti-Semites who objected to his interference. Zola was buried in the cemetery in Montmartre. Although his grave can still be seen, his remains were removed and he was reburied with honor in 1908 in the Panthéon, alongside France's other literary greats.

ANATOLE FRANCE

Zola's funeral in Montmartre attracted vast crowds. One speaker who addressed the mourners was fellow writer Anatole France. France was regarded at the time as the best writer of the era: Zola's equal, if not superior. His work brought him more honors than Zola received. France was elected to l'Académie française in 1896, and he was awarded the Nobel Prize for Literature in 1921.

Anatole France had been born in Paris in 1844. His father was a bookseller, one of the *bouquinistes* (second-hand booksellers) whose stalls can still be seen today along the quais of the River Seine, and the young France was an avid reader from his childhood onward. His father wanted him to become a bookseller, but the boy wanted to be a book writer instead. France was 29 when he published his first book, a collection of verses called *Les poèmes dorés* (*The Golden Poems*). France failed to reach a wide audience until his first novel, *Le crime de Sylvestre Bonnard* (*The Crime of Sylvestre Bonnard*), published in 1881 when France was 37. By the standards of the other great writers of the time, France had a later start than most.

Despite the late start, France went on to produce a considerable volume of work, including poetry, plays, articles, and essays. He also wrote contemporary and historical novels. France was truly a man of letters. Alongside Zola, France also supported the battle to find out the truth of the Dreyfus Affair, and he later wrote a series of four novels, *L'Histoire contemporaine* (*A Contemporary Story*), in which he examined the importance of the affair and the effect it had on French life. The last of these novels, *Monsieur Bergeret à Paris* (*Monsieur Bergeret in Paris*), was an autobiographical tale in which Monsieur Bergeret, a thoughtful man of letters, was drawn onto the public stage because of the Dreyfus Affair, just as Anatole France had been.

When he was successful and his literary earnings had become considerable, France bought a house in Neuilly. It is to the west of the city center and is still an attractive neighborhood today. France died in 1924 and is buried in the cemetery at Neuilly.

THE SYMBOLIST MOVEMENT

Anatole France's writing very much harked back to the classical tradition, yet at the same time in Paris a very different style of writing was developing: the symbolist movement. Three of its main proponents were Stéphane Mallarmé, Paul Verlaine, and

Arthur Rimbaud. These three names are inextricably linked together, but the friendship was not always harmonious.

It was not simply the use of symbols that make their writing new; rather, it was their heavy reliance on imagery and reverie to reflect the events of the world. In Paris in the late 19th century, symbolism became a strong movement for writers and artists alike. They did not want the romantic writing of Victor Hugo, the intellectual classicism of Anatole France, or the gritty realism of Émile Zola. The symbolists believed in using imagination, fantasy, dreams, and symbols to express what was going on in their own lives and in the world around them.

Nerval and Baudelaire had already paved the way, earlier in the century, but the movement really took off in the later period when Paris was a thriving community of writers and artists, stimulating one other, working together, arguing and debating. The places in Paris most closely associated with the symbolists are the places where most of this debating raged: the cafés.

Cafés had always been a central part of Parisian artistic and intellectual life, ever since Le Procope had first opened its doors in 1686. Two hundred years later, Mallarmé, Verlaine, and Rimbaud were meeting there, at 13 rue de l'Ancienne-Comédie. The three would also meet at the Deux Magots café, 6 place St-Germain-des-Prés, which would really come into its own as a haunt of writers in the 20th century, and still opens its doors from dawn until the early hours of the morning every day. Another favorite spot was the venerable Café Voltaire at 1 place de l'Odéon, which had been named for Voltaire who had met there with Diderot in the 18th century.

Mallarmé had been born in Paris in 1842, learned English at the Lycée Fontane, and like Baudelaire before him, translated the work of Edgar Allan Poe into French. Mallarmé's best-known poem is "L'Après-midi d'un faune" ("The Afternoon of a Faun"), which was published in 1876 and later inspired the French composer Claude Debussy to write the symphonic work called *Prélude à l'après-midi d'un faune* (*Prelude to the Afternoon of a Faun*) in 1894. Mallarmé's total output was small, but his was influence considerable. He was a great speaker and inspiration for others at the regular "Tuesday evenings" that Mallarmé organized. He died in 1898 in Valvins, a small and peaceful village by the River Seine about 40 miles (64 km) south of Paris, where the poet had a country cottage.

Another influential member of the symbolist movement was Paul Verlaine. He was born in 1844 in Metz, in eastern France, into a military family. Verlaine came to Paris when he was quite young and attended the Lycée Bonaparte, where he first displayed his precocious talent. At the age of 14, he wrote a poem called "Le mort" ("Death") and sent it to Victor Hugo for his opinion. At 19, Verlaine published his first poem and was already frequenting the cafés where he would meet writers such as Mallarmé and France.

At age 26, with a few published collections to his name, Verlaine married. Only two years later, he left his wife, choosing instead to live and travel with the young poet Arthur Rimbaud. The following year, the two had a drunken argument and Verlaine shot Rimbaud in the arm. Verlaine was imprisoned for two years. The statement he made about his crime is on display at the Musée des Collections Historiques de la Préfecture de Police (Police Museum) at 1 bis rue des Carmes.

While in prison, Verlaine wrote his collection *Romances sans paroles* (*Songs Without Words*) in 1874. It was about his life with Rimbaud. Verlaine also took up again the Catholicism of his youth, and the rest of his life was made up of swings between drunken debauchery and repentance. He died in 1896 in the Latin Quarter at 39 rue Descartes. The building later became a cheap hotel where in 1922 a hopeful young American writer named Ernest Hemingway would rent a room. Today, it is an apartment building. A statue to Verlaine can be found in the Luxembourg Gardens.

The third founding member of the symbolist movement was Arthur Rimbaud. Rimbaud was born in Charleville in 1854. As a young man, Rimbaud had sent some of his poems to Verlaine. At the age of 17, Rimbaud moved to Paris at the invitation of

Verlaine. The two began their stormy relationship, with one of Rimbaud's poems of the time being called appropriately, "Le bateau ivre" ("The Drunken Boat"). The title was a perfect mix of the symbolic and the real in describing their life together, and it is regarded as one of Rimbaud's best works. After Verlaine had been imprisoned, Rimbaud wrote *Une saison en enfer* (*A Season in Hell*).

In 1874, Rimbaud moved to England. There, he taught French and wrote some poems that Verlaine published in a literary magazine he was involved with. From then on, though, Rimbaud wrote nothing more, but went off traveling through Europe, North Africa, and the Middle East. He only returned to France at the very end of his life, and he died from a brain tumor in 1891.

HENRY JAMES

The work of the writer Henry James could hardly be more different from that of the symbolist poets. James wrote novels of meticulous detail, investigating the psychological depths of his characters in the context of more thinly structured plots. James had been born in the United States in 1843, and he spent most of his life in England. Despite this, James spent a lot of time in Paris and wrote books that were set there, such as *The American* in 1877, and *The Ambassadors* in 1903.

James first came to Paris as a young boy with his family, and as a 12-year-old he lived at the Hôtel Westminster, 13 rue de la Paix. He then moved to 19 rue de la Boétie for a year, and then when he was 14 he lived at 26 avenue Montaigne. James's father was a philosopher and theologian who provided his son with a love of travel and of Europe. The young Henry James returned to the United States to study at Harvard, and he soon began writing. Paris was not far from his mind, however, and he returned to the city on a visit in 1872. At that time, he met the Bostonian poet Ralph Waldo Emerson at the home of another Bostonian poet, James Russell Lowell, who was living then at 7 rue de Beaune.

Henry James moved to Paris in November 1875. At this point, he had already had his first novel published and was highly praised for his short stories. Now, while in Paris, he was working as a correspondent for the *New York Tribune*. He took an apartment at 29 rue Cambon, and it was while living there that he started to work on his first novel set in Paris, *The American*, which was published in 1877. The novel tells the story of an American millionaire who comes to Paris and attempts to marry the daughter of a family of French aristocrats. In the process, the novel explores the cultural differences between the two nations.

In Paris, James quickly became a part of the literary scene, and met writers including Flaubert, Zola, and Maupassant, as well as the Russian Ivan Turgenev who spent his later years in Paris. Like other authors, James also mingled with the city's leading artists. By the 1890s, the Massachusetts-born painter James McNeill Whistler had an apartment at 110 rue du Bac, where James would visit him and meet Parisian-based artists such as Manet, Dégas, and Toulouse-Lautrec. By this time, James was no longer living in the city, but he was a frequent visitor from his new base in London, about 200 miles (322 km) from Paris across the English Channel.

Although James had left Paris physically, he returned to the theme of Paris in his writing with *The Ambassadors*, which was published in 1903. In this novel, as in *The American*, an American man comes to Paris but this time he is middle-aged. The man is not looking not for a wife but rather a rich young American man whose family members think has spent too long overseas. It is the job of "the ambassador" to persuade him to return home. Instead, the ambassador himself feels increasingly warm towards the civilized life he finds in Paris. It is very different from not only his expectations, but also the restraints of his own life at home on the east coast. Paris had seduced another visitor.

OSCAR WILDE

Americans, especially artists and writers like James and Emerson, were now starting to visit the city in large numbers. Paris seemed to have a particular appeal to Irish writers, too. The first notable Irish literary figure to visit the city was Oscar Wilde. He moved to the city in 1897, having been persecuted in England for his homosexuality and sentenced to two years in prison in 1895. He had been at the height of his career, having published his novel *The Picture of Dorian Gray* in 1891, and then in quick succession his plays *Lady Windermere's Fan* in 1892, *A Woman of No Importance* in 1893, and *The Importance of Being Earnest* in 1895.

After fleeing to France, Wilde would only publish one more work, though this would be the most powerful poem he ever wrote, "The Ballad of Reading Gaol," which was published in 1898. While in Paris, Wilde is known to have visited the Café de la Paix at 1 place de l'Opéra and the Grand Café Capucines at 4 boulevard des Capucines. He stayed for a time at the Hôtel du Quai Voltaire, 19 quai Voltaire, which is still a hotel today.

Although he spent time in the city's cafés and the Hôtel du Quai, the Parisian place most associated with Wilde is the place where he died. Now called simply L'Hôtel (The Hotel), in Wilde's day it was called the Hôtel d'Alsace, 13 rue des Beaux-Arts in St-Germain. The author's death, given his flamboyant and dramatic life, was poignantly low-key. In 1900, he caught an ear infection and contracted meningitis, and he died in his hotel room. Wilde was renowned for his pithy and witty remarks: once, a customs officer asked him if he had anything to declare and he is said to have responded: "I have nothing to declare but my genius." Different accounts attribute different last words to him. One account has him saying, "I am dying beyond my means," while the more popular version of his final words has him looking at his rather cheap hotel room and declaring, "Either that wallpaper goes, or I do." Whatever the case, the hotel room can still be rented, though the wallpaper has since been changed.

GEORGES FEYDEAU AND ANDRÉ GIDE

Paris at this time had its own witty dramatist, in the shape of Georges Feydeau. Born in Paris in 1862, he is still regarded as the funniest French playwright since Molière. Like Molière, he began both acting and writing from an early age. He was incredibly prolific, writing at least one full-length play a year for most of his working life. The plays were broad farces with exaggerated stock characters and lots of confusion. They poked fun at the pretensions of Parisian society and its embrace of every new trend that came along. Feydeau's best-known works include *La dame de chez Maxim* (*The Girl from Maxim's*) written in 1899 and *La puce à l'oreille* (*A Flea in Her Ear*) written in 1907. They were, and still are, performed at the Comédie-Française, the theater founded by the actors in Molière's troop after his death. The theater can be found at 2 rue de Richelieu.

The farces of Feydeau are quite a contrast to the contemporaneous philosophical dramas, novels, and literary criticisms of André Gide. Gide was born in Paris in 1869, and educated at the École Alsacienne and the Lycée Henri IV. He had published his first book by the time he was 22. Gide was friendly with the symbolist writers and attended Mallarmé's "Tuesday evenings" for a time, although his own work was always far too individualistic to fit into any movement. He was encouraged by Oscar Wilde, and was a fellow habitué of the Café de la Paix and a regular visitor to yet another literary haunt, the Brasserie Lipp at 151 boulevard St-Germain.

Gide's 1926 novel *Les faux-monnayeurs* (*The Counterfeiters*) deals with the lives of a group of schoolboys in Paris at that time, and the four volumes of his *Journal* also naturally include much material about his life and that of other writers in the city. His apartment at 1 bis rue Vaneau became a salon where writers of the day would gather. In 1947, he was awarded the Nobel Prize for Literature, and he died in Paris in 1951.

SIDONIE-GABRIELLE COLETTE

One writer whose work captures the mood and flavor of the

Paris of her time is Colette. Sidonie-Gabrielle Colette was born in Burgundy in 1873. She married a writer named Henri Gauthier-Villars when she was 20 years old and moved with him to Paris. The two of them collaborated on a series of novels, but it was later revealed that these four semi-autobiographical fictions about a woman named Claudine were largely the work of Colette alone. She wrote many more novels featuring female characters, often loosely based on herself. The best-known of these novels was the 1945 story, *Gigi*, which was later turned into a successful film that won the Academy Award for Best Motion Picture in 1958.

Colette did not live to see the movie and its success. She died in Paris in 1954. She had lived much of her life in an apartment at 9 rue de Beaujolais, overlooking the Palais-Royal. She was always a stylish woman, and dined regularly at the nearby high-class restaurant, Le Grand Véfour, and it is said that she died with a glass of champagne in her hand. She is buried in the cemetery at Père-Lachaise.

MARCEL PROUST

Buried at Père-Lachaise, too, is perhaps the most important French writer of the early 20th century: Marcel Proust. Reading Proust's long, brilliant novel—like reading *War and Peace, Moby Dick,* and *Ulysses*—is high on the list of aspirations for many literature lovers.

Marcel Proust was born in Paris in 1871. Proust's father was an eminent doctor, and his family was respectable and prosperous. When Proust was a child, his family lived in the house at 9 place de la Madeleine. At the age of eight Proust had his first asthma attack, and he was dogged by ill health all his life. As a young man, Proust studied law. He had no real need to earn a living, however, and he spent some time being a man-about-town in Parisian society. He also started to write. His first work was a mixture of stories and essays, published when he was 25. Proust also spent time campaigning on behalf of the imprisoned Alfred Dreyfus.

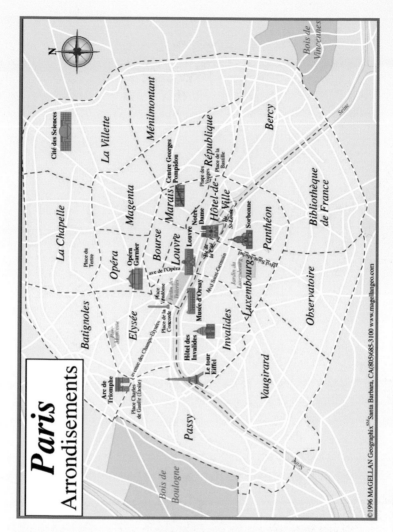

■ The Péipherique is the ring-like road that surrounds the city of Paris. Within this boundary, the city is divided into 20 sections or neighborhoods called Arrondissements. The Arrondissements are numbered starting in the center and rotating clockwise outward. During the 19th century the landscape and layout of the city underwent drastic changes at the hands of Baron Georges Eugène Haussmann. Baron Haussmann is credited with remodeling the ancient city in favor of the now famous broad avenues that intersect the city today.

■ Among the more significant events in French history is the storming of the Bastille. Indeed, July 14th recognized as Bastille Day is the French national holiday marking the country's independence. Originally built as a fortification against the British, the Bastille functioned as a state-run prison. The Marquis de Sade and Voltaire were some of the famous writers imprisoned there.

■ Theater flourished under the rule of Louis XIV in the 17th century. Jean Baptiste Poquelin, better known as Molière, was the great comic playwright of the day. Born in 1622 Molière gained fame for his satires that depicted the everyday foibles of the growing middle class. It is Molière's troupe that formed the basis of Comédie Francaise, the state theater of France.

■ This illustration depicts the scene of Voltaire's arrest by order of Frederick II. Voltaire was no stranger to exile and arrest having been sentenced to the Bastille twice, and forced into exile after being released from his second imprisonment. Many of Voltaire's troubles, including his arrest by Fredrick II, arose from his inflammatory writings.

■ Despite living significant portions of his life in exile from Paris, the city later recognized and adopted Voltaire as one of their literary greats, and Voltaire returned to the city at age 83 to much fanfare. In 1791, Voltaire's remains were moved to the Pantheon but his heart, however had long since been removed from his body, and is seen here being placed in a statue at the Bibliotheque Nationale in Paris.

■ Honoré de Balzac was one of France's most prolific writers. His massive output of novels and short stories are collected under the title *La Comédie humaine,* yet despite these efforts, Balzac spent much of his life in debt. The Balzac Museum, pictured above, is the only one of Balzac's several residences still standing.

■ Marcel Proust, famous for his masterwork of modern fiction *Á la Recherche du temps perdu*, spent much of his life in and around Paris, and indeed wrote about the city in his work. Proust's writing influenced many authors around the world including James Joyce and Virginia Woolf. Proust died in 1922 and is buried in the often-visited Père-Lachaise cemetery.

■ It wasn't until the author Victor Hugo wrote about Notre-Dame in his famous novel *Notre-Dame de Paris* that this cathedral, then in a state of severe disrepair, was rescued from near destruction. Construction on this gothic master-piece was begun in 1163 and finished in 1345.

■ Initially built as a fortification and used as a royal palace, the Louvre was inaugurated as the Musée Central des Arts in 1793. It is now a world-renowned museum, and many of the works contained within have proven inspirational to countless writers and poets. The glass pyramid at the front serves as a grand entrance and was designed by I.M. Pei.

■ The largest arch of its kind, the Arc de Triomphe stands an impressive164 feet (50 m) high and 147 feet (45 m) wide, and was modeled after the ancient triumphal arches of Rome. Commissioned by Napoléon as a monument to the French military, the arch has served as the symbolic center of the city of Paris.

■ Few monuments in Paris caused as much controversy as the Eiffel Tower. In protest of the tower, 300 artists signed and published a petition. The tower was considered to be a monstrosity by a number of artists: a "truly tragic street lamp" (Léon Bloy), "belfry skeleton" (Paul Verlaine). After leaving Paris, Guy de Maupassant maintained the claim that he left to escape the Eiffel Tower.

■ Perhaps more so than any other city, Paris has come to epitomize sidewalk café culture. The famous left bank is dotted with well-known and revered cafés including Brasserie Lipp, Café de Flore, and Les Deux Magots. North of the city center is the famous Café de la Paix. Among the café's writerly clientele were Émile Zola, Guy de Maupassant, Oscar Wilde, and Ernest Hemingway.

■ Contributing to the legend of the city's café culture, painter Georges Croegaert immortalized the Café de la Paix in his painting *At the Café de la Paix* (1883). During the 19th century, the Café and the nearby opera house, Opéra Garnier, were the center of elegant society.

When he was 35, Proust fell seriously ill. He then retreated to a cork-lined room that he rarely left. By 1905, he was spending all his time working on what would be his masterwork. It would become a multi-volume series called *À la recherche du temps perdu* (usually translated as *Remembrance of Things Past*).

Proust wrote and rewrote sections of the book, putting it down, writing other things, then returning to it. He finished the first volume, *Du côté de chez Swann* (*Swann's Way*), in 1912. It was published the following year at his own expense, and it attracted little attention. In 1919, the second volume appeared, and the reaction was totally different. It was received with great acclaim and won the most prestigious French literary prize, the Prix Goncourt. Other volumes came out at the rate of one a year, and when Proust died of pneumonia in 1922, there were three volumes written but still not published.

Proust died in his apartment at 14 rue Hamelin on the boulevard Haussmann, which was named after the architect whose sweeping changes had altered the entire face of Paris. It was an appropriate address for the man whose vast novel swept across the entire face of Paris, capturing life among the upper and upper-middle classes in particular. The intricacies of Paris's social world, together with the beauty of its architecture, afforded Proust an endless array of details to fuel his meditative imaginings and comedic discernments, as here in *The Guermantes Way*.

Then, after Saint-Loup had told me various anecdotes about his cousin's chaplain, her gardeners and the rest, the Hôtel de Guermantes had become—as the Louvre might have been in days gone by—a kind of palace surrounded, in the very heart of Paris, by its own domains, acquired by inheritance, by virtue of an ancient right that had quaintly survived, over which she still enjoyed feudal privileges. But this last dwelling had itself vanished when we came to live near Mme de Guermantes ... It was one of those old town houses, a few of which for all I know may still be found, in which the main

courtyard was flanked—alluvial deposits washed there by the
rising tide of democracy, perhaps, or a legacy from a more
primitive time when the different trades were clustered round
the overlord—by little shops and work-rooms, a shoemaker's,
for instance, or a tailor's, such as we see nestling between the
buttresses of those cathedrals which the aesthetic zeal of the
restorer has not swept clear of such accretions ... and, at the
far end, in the main house, a "Countess" who, when she
drove out in her old carriage and pair, flaunting on her hat a
few nasturtiums which seemed to have escaped from the plot
by the lodge ... dispensed smiles and little waves of the hand
impartially to the porter's children and to any bourgeois ten-
ants who might happen to be passing and whom, in her dis-
dainful affability and her egalitarian arrogance, she found
indistinguishable from one another. (10–11)

The narrator's mentality contrasts with that of the
"Countess," who is incapable of distinguishing people from one
another: the narrator is endlessly open to the revelation of each
change and shift, and seems capable of distinguishing everything, not just people, from everything. Proust's tragicomic
genius found its proper *materia poetica* in the byzantine com-
plexities of Paris's people and history.

CHAPTER | **EIGHT**

Between the Wars

In Marcel Proust's last days, a young American arrived in Paris with dreams of being a writer. In contrast to Proust's multi-volume work that was filled with sensitive detail and sumptuous sentences, this new arrival would turn the literary world upside down with his determination to write stark, simple, tough prose. His name was Ernest Hemingway.

AMERICAN EXPATRIATES IN PARIS

Hemingway was born in Illinois in 1899. As a young man, he obtained a job as a reporter on the *Kansas City Star* newspaper. He then left to volunteer as an ambulance driver in the First World War. Hemingway was not a modest man, and his own accounts of his involvement in the First World War—not to mention the Second World War—need to be taken with a pinch of salt, if not a whole packet. In his own eyes, he came close to winning both wars almost single-handedly. The truth, however, is harder to determine because there are several contradictory accounts of his exploits. Indeed, Hemingway's own accounts were sometimes contradictory.

What is not in dispute is the author's impact on the world of literature. His writing style was new, and he went on to create classic works such as *The Old Man and the Sea*, *To Have and Have Not*, and *For Whom the Bell Tolls*. He would eventually win the Nobel Prize for Literature. Before he had theses successes, however, Hemingway lived through many years of struggle and poverty. His great nonfiction book, *A Moveable Feast*, tells of Hemingway's time in Paris during his early years as a writer. He was a penniless, struggling author who on occasion was reduced to catching pigeons in Luxembourg Garden in order to have something to eat. That is, at least, according to Hemingway.

The young American had arrived in Paris in 1921, at the age of 22. He was a reporter for the *Toronto Star*, but his occasional pieces were far from enough to earn a decent living. He spent his first night in the city in room number 14 at the Hôtel d'Angleterre, 44 rue Jacob, which is still in existence. Rooms today, however, cost considerably more than they did in Hemingway's time, when the hotel offered a much more basic living arrangement.

Hemingway then took a room on the top floor of another cheap hotel at 39 rue Descartes, the same hotel where Paul Verlaine had died in 1896. A plaque marks the poet's death, and another sign says that Hemingway lived there from 1921 to 1925. In truth, however, Hemingway moved out of the hotel in 1922 and took his first apartment in Paris around the corner at 74 rue du Cardinal-Lemoine. By then, Hemingway had married his first wife, Hadley, and *A Moveable Feast* gives a vivid account of their time there together.

Paris represents many things to many people, but the Paris Hemingway describes in the opening pages of *A Moveable Feast* may represent what more people wish to find there than any other writing about Paris written since, the elegant pathos of his threadbare existence there and the wet weather notwithstanding:

All of the sadness of the city came suddenly with the first cold rains of winter, and there were no more tops to the high white houses as you walked but only the wet blackness of the street and the closed doors of the small shops, the herb sellers, the stationery and newspaper shops, the midwife—second class—and the hotel where Verlaine had died where I had a room on the top floor where I worked. (4)

The thought of his room reminds him of his need for firewood to warm it, and his lack of the money to buy it, so he walks on:

I walked down past the Lycée Henri Quatre and the ancient church of St.-Etienne-du-Mont and the windswept Place du Panthéon and cut in for shelter to the right and finally came out on the lee side of the Boulevard St.-Michel and worked on down it past the Cluny and the Boulevard St.-Germain until I came to a good café that I knew on the Place St.-Michel. It was a pleasant café, warm and clean and friendly, and I hung up my old waterproof on the coat rack to dry and put my worn and weathered felt hat on the rack above the bench and ordered a café au lait. The waiter brought it and I took out a notebook from the pocket of the coat and a pencil and started to write. (5)

After the *café au lait*, he drinks a rum St. James. After that he sees a beautiful girl and ruminates about the power he has over Paris and its inhabitants through his internal writing life: "You belong to me and all Paris belongs to me and I belong to this notebook and this pencil." Then comes another rum St. James, he is completely absorbed in his writing. Soon the story is finished, he switches from rum to white wine and oysters; he is "sure this was a very good story although I would not know truly how good until I read it over the next day" (6). Such is the popularity of the book that the details related here, taken as a group, are sure to seem a bit clichéd—the pennilessness, the *café au lait*, the beautiful mysterious girl, the notebook—though probably they are true to Hemingway's experience. Would-be writers had sought nice Parisian cafés in which to write their masterpieces before Hemingway; after Hemingway, they have had to do so with the subtle awareness that they are following his example. At the heart of the romantic solitude he enjoys here is a sense of freedom—the girl and the whole city belong to him, while he belongs solely to his art.

Hemingway quickly fell in with other expatriate Americans already living in Paris, most notably Ezra Pound and Gertrude Stein. Pound and Stein were famous and influential, and they encouraged the young author who would eventually eclipse both of them with his fame, respect, and popularity.

Gertrude Stein was an influence on many young writers, especially Americans, who were arriving in Paris in increasing numbers. The First World War had introduced many of them to life in Europe. Paris, in particular, was seen as liberating and exotic, romantic and bohemian. These notions had been fueled by tales of the sometimes-reckless lives of the city's impressionist artists and surrealist poets of the late 19th century.

Stein, who was born in Pennsylvania in 1874, had arrived in Paris in 1903. Apart from a temporary exile in the countryside during the Nazi occupation of Second World War, she would live all her life in Paris with her partner, Alice B. Toklas. From 1903 to 1938, Stein lived at 27 rue de Fleurus, at first with her brother and then with Toklas. Their home was a literary magnet to residents and visitors alike, and any American writer who spent time in Paris during those years probably visited them at this address.

In 1938, Stein and Toklas were evicted from their longtime home, and they moved to 5 rue Christine in St-Germain. They would not stay there long, however, before the Nazi occupation of Paris caused them to retreat to the countryside. After Paris was liberated, they returned to the city. Stein died in 1946, and Toklas lived on at 5 rue Christine until her death in 1967. Today, the two are still companions, buried alongside each other in the cemetery at Père-Lachaise.

Stein's deliberately difficult prose-style ensured that she

would never have the popular fame that later came to Hemingway. Her best-known book is *The Autobiography of Alice B. Toklas*, which was published in 1933. Despite what the title suggests, the book was, in fact, Stein's own autobiography. In it, she includes an account of her long and sometime difficult friendship with Hemingway. Alongside this, it is fascinating to read Hemingway's own version of the same events as presented in *A Moveable Feast*.

By 1926, Hemingway had published one book of stories and poems, and another collection of stories, and in that year he published the novel that would make his name, *The Sun Also Rises*. Parts of this are set in Paris, with fictionalized versions of himself and some of the people he knew there. Parts of the book are also set in Spain, where Hemingway loved to travel and which would appear in his later works, including his 1932 book about bullfighting, *Death in the Afternoon*.

Paris remained Hemingway's base on and off for several years, although he also spent time fighting in the Spanish Civil War in the late 1930s and the Second World War in the early 1940s. While in Paris, however, he enjoyed visiting his friend Sylvia Beach who was living at 93 boulevard St-Michel at the time. Beach was the founder of the famous Shakespeare and Company bookshop. It was originally located at 12 rue de l'Odéon, but has since moved to 37 rue de la Bûcherie. Shakespeare and Company was more than just a bookshop, however. It acted as an unofficial lending library to struggling writers like Hemingway, who would borrow books they could not afford to buy and then return them to the shop shelves. The shop was also a meeting place where readings were held, and eventually the shop published books, too.

Hemingway himself was first published in Paris by the Three Mountains Press. It was the publishing house where the poet Ezra Pound—who was a great promoter of Hemingway's work—had a job as an editor. The press had its offices at 29 quai d'Anjou on the Île St-Louis, while Pound himself lived for a time in the Hôtel Élysée, 9 rue de Beaune.

There are many other Parisian sites associated with Hemingway, as you would expect from the many years he lived in the city. Many of these sites are bars, cafés, and restaurants. They including the Polidor Bistro at 41 rue Monsieur-le-Prince; the Brasserie Lipp at 151 boulevard St-Germain; La Closerie des Lilas, where Hemingway would frequently sit and write, at 171 boulevard du Montparnasse; Harry's New York Bar at 5 rue Daunou; and, of course, the cafés where every writer and artist went, Les Deux Magots at 6 place St-Germain-des-Prés and the Café de Flore at 172 boulevard St-Germain.

Other sites in Paris are also closely associated with Hemingway. The author had lived for a time, in 1924, in an apartment at 113 rue Notre-Dame-des-Champs. Spanish artist Pablo Picasso had a studio at 7 rue des Grand Augustins, where Hemingway visited him in 1946. Perhaps the address best associated with Hemingway, however, is an entire street: rue Mouffetard. This market street still retains its traditional atmosphere, though the area is much more fashionable now than it was in Hemingway's day. He loved the street and its nearby cafés, and it is vividly described in *A Moveable Feast.*

Hemingway's final permanent address in Paris was at 6 rue Férou. It was a hotel he moved into in 1926 after he had left his wife Hadley for a *Vogue* journalist named Pauline Pfeiffer, who would later become his second wife. By that point, Hemingway was on his way to fame and wealth, and his new wife was independently rich, so he no more would live in cheap hotel rooms with cold water and a bathroom down the hall.

If Hemingway's name was the biggest on the list of American writers in Paris, it was far from being the only one. His sometime friend and sometime rival, F. Scott Fitzgerald, was another American author who made Paris his home for a while. Like Hemingway, Fitzgerald frequently visited the Ritz Hotel's bar and borrowed the hotel's name for one of his best-known short stories, "The Diamond as Big as the Ritz."

During his own brief stay in Paris, Fitzgerald was rather too fond of spending time in bars like the one at the Ritz, and quickly gained a reputation for his drunken behavior. He had friends in the Paris office of the *Chicago Tribune* newspaper— including author James Thurber, who became known for his humorous books—who would often have to take the drunken Fitzgerald home to his apartment. During this time, Fitzgerald lived at 14 rue de Tilsitt with his wife, Zelda, and their daughter, Scottie.

Few of Fitzgerald's works are set in Paris, but another American author, Henry Miller, made the city the focus of several of his novels. Miller was born in New York in 1891 and moved to Paris in 1930. He was a notorious womanizer, and he used his own adventures in the city's bohemian underworld as the setting for novels such as *Tropic of Cancer* in 1934 and *Tropic of Capricorn* in 1939. The explicit novels were banned in the United States, Britain, and many other countries. In Paris, however, a small publishing house called the Obelisk Press, located at 16 place Vendôme, agreed to publish the books. The two books were not published in the United States until 1961.

Miller lived in Paris for just ten years before returning to the United States in 1940. Before moving to Paris permanently, Miller had spent the spring of 1928 in the city in an apartment at 24 rue Bonaparte. When he moved to Paris in 1930, he took a room on the top floor of the Hôtel St-Germain-des-Pres at number 36 on the same street, which is still a hotel today. Later, while writing the notorious *Tropic of Cancer* and *Tropic of Capricorn*, he would drink and work at the Hôtel Pont Royal, 5–7 rue Montalemert. Miller is also known to have frequented the La Palette café at 43 rue de Seine, as well as the usual American literary haunts including Shakespeare and Company— although unlike Hemingway, Miller is said to have kept the books he borrowed from the bookshop's unofficial library.

PARISIAN AUTHORS

Although these American expatriate writers mixed with each other in the cafés and bookshops, they were using the same cafés that Parisian writers and artists frequented, and many of them socialized together. French writing was as vigorous as it had always been. One French native who embraced the world of writing—as well as the worlds of painting, filmmaking, and acting—was Jean Cocteau.

Cocteau had been born in 1889 in Maisons-Laffitte, on the northwestern outskirts of Paris. He was not especially good in school and dropped out. Despite this lack of formal education, by the age of 19 Cocteau had published his first book of poetry, *La lampe d'Aladin* (*Aladdin's Lamp*), which was well received. In the same year, 1909, he met the famous Russian ballet producer Sergei Diaghilev, who was in Paris with the Russian Ballet, and the versatile Cocteau produced two ballet scenarios.

During the First World War Cocteau had worked, like Hemingway, as an ambulance driver. He became acquainted with several of the most outstanding writers and artists of the day, including Pablo Picasso, Amedeo Modigliani, and Guillaume Apollinaire. Along with Apollinaire, Cocteau was a leading light in the surrealist movement, and he continued to produce a wide range of works across several art forms. His best-known play is *Orphée* (*Orpheus*), which was first performed in 1926 and was later turned into a film. It tells the story of a Parisian poet whose work is derided by his Left Bank contemporaries, so he seeks inspiration through a mysterious princess who leads him into the underworld of the dead.

Les enfants terribles was a novel that Cocteau wrote in three weeks in 1929, and which he would also later turn into a highly acclaimed film. It is a work whose title is usually not rendered into English, where the equivalent phrase, *The Terrible Children*, certainly loses something in translation. It tells the tale of two Parisian adolescents, a brother and sister, who create their own surreal fantasy world after the death of their mother.

The most interesting Parisian location connected with Cocteau is the Hôtel de Biron at 77 rue de Varenne. This was a collection of artists' studios, and Cocteau used one of them alongside other artists, including the German poet Rainer Maria Rilke, the French painter Henri Matisse, and the American dancer Isadora Duncan. The most famous inhabitant, however, was the sculptor Auguste Rodin, and the house has been converted into the Rodin Museum, which is an essential place to visit on any trip to Paris. Cocteau would also meet with the other surrealists at Le Boeuf sur le Toit, a 1930s Art Deco brasserie that can still be found at 34 rue du Colisée.

A near contemporary of the sometimes shocking Cocteau was the eminently respectable André Malraux, one of the few

Rodin Museum

The Rodin Museum includes one rather startling exhibit for the literary visitor: a huge, nude statue of the writer Honoré de Balzac. Auguste Rodin did several studies of the author in the 1890s when he was commissioned to create a statue of Balzac for public display. Balzac died in 1850, so the works were not done from life. Several of the efforts are shown in the museum, and the final version of the statue, in which the author is wearing a cloak, was erected in boulevard Raspail, near the junction with boulevard du Montparnasse. Rodin also sculpted Victor Hugo, and this statue can also be viewed in the Rodin Museum alongside examples of many of the artist's famous works including *The Thinker, The Kiss, The Gates of Hell,* and *The Burghers of Calais.*

The museum is housed in the Hôtel Biron, which was built in 1730 as a private residence. It later served as a school until 1904, when it was divided up into artists' studios that were rented out by the government. The most famous artist to rent a studio here was Rodin, although he did not so much pay the rent as owe the rent. When he died in 1917, he left many of his works to the French nation, in lieu of the rent that he owed, for which we must all now be grateful. The house and its gardens are one of the most delightful museums in Paris.

writers who can be said to have physically changed the face of Paris through his later work as a politician and minister of culture. In 1964, Malraux was responsible for designating the Marais as the first historic preservation district in Paris, an action that started the area's regeneration after it had fallen into disrepair. Malraux also commissioned the works of art that adorn the courtyards of the Palais-Royal, partly because his office windows overlooked them and he wanted something aesthetically pleasing that both he and the pubic could enjoy. His home was for many years at 44 rue du Bac on the Left Bank.

Malraux was a Parisian through and through. He was born in the city in 1901 to a respectable and wealthy family, and he studied at Paris's School of Oriental Languages. He then traveled for some time in Asia, and wrote about it in his novels. The best known of these works is *La condition humaine* (*The Human Condition*), which was published in 1933. It won France's greatest literary prize, Le Prix Goncourt, and went on to be translated into many languages.

Malraux fought in the French Resistance Movement during the German occupation of Paris in the Second World War. He then went on to serve for many years as minister of culture under President Charles de Gaulle. Malraux continued to write and to be active in the architectural and cultural development of the city until his death in 1976.

JAMES JOYCE

Malraux was perhaps the archetypal French writer—an intellectual, a soldier, an adventurer, and a politician. Yet Paris also appealed to writers who lived very different lives, such as Irish author James Joyce, one of the greatest writers of the 20th century.

Joyce was born in Dublin in 1882 and first came to Paris as a medical student, though he had to return home early when his mother became ill. He spent most of his life in self-imposed exile in France and Italy. Yet from these locations, Joyce produced perhaps the most remarkable book ever written about the city of his childhood and youth in his novel *Ulysses*.

In 1920, Joyce was living in Trieste in northeastern Italy. Ezra Pound persuaded Joyce and his wife, Nora, to come to Paris and join the thriving literary scene there, which Pound believed would be more open-minded and receptive to Joyce's rather challenging and unconventional work. At the time, Pound was living at 9 rue de Beaune in St-Germain, and arranged for the Joyces to stay at an inexpensive hotel a few streets away at 9 rue de l'Université. It was the same place where the British-based American poet T.S. Eliot spent the summer of 1910, several years before his first collection was published. Today this location is the chic and considerably more expensive Lenox Hotel.

Joyce achieved his greatest fame in Paris, which is where his work *Ulysses* was first published. *Ulysses* tells the story of one day in the life of Dubliner Leopold Bloom, a Jewish advertising salesman, in a stream-of-consciousness fashion. Many of the book's passages were regarded as obscene and as a result, the book was considered too shocking for publication. Although no conventional publisher would consider the book, Sylvia Beach of Shakespeare and Company believed in this work by Joyce, just as she believed in many of the authors who frequented her bookshop. In 1922, Beach brought out the first edition of *Ulysses*. Today, many critics regarded it as the greatest novel of the 20th century. As proof, a copy of Joyce's first edition of *Ulysses* recently sold at auction for almost $500,000, and sections of Joyce's original manuscript pages fetch more than $1 million.

At the time *Ulysses* was published, however, Joyce was short of money. For a while, he shared an apartment with the French author Valéry Larbaud at 51 rue de la Montagne-Ste-Geneviéve, close to the Panthéon. The respected Larbaud gave a lecture about *Ulysses* upon the book's publication, which helped it to become an immediate success. Joyce became a fixture on the Paris literary scene, but he always remained an intensely private man. A gregarious Hemingway or politician like Malraux, he was not.

Joyce stayed in Paris while working on his next novel,

Finnegans Wake. It was a work so dense that it would make *Ulysses* seem like an easy read. *Finnegans Wake* would occupy the author until it was published in 1939. From 1935 to 1939, the Joyces lives at 7 rue Edmond-Valentin, not far from the Eiffel Tower. After 20 years in the city, Joyce eventually left Paris in 1940 when France fell to Germany during the Second World War. He returned with his family to the safety of Switzerland, and died there in 1941.

GEORGES SIMENON

It had taken Joyce some 17 years to complete his final monumental novel, *Finnegans Wake*. This stands in stark contrast with the prolific output of a very different type of author, Georges Simenon. Simenon would certainly have written several hundred books in that same period. Born in Belgium in 1903, Simenon came to Paris in 1922 and was determined to be a writer. For him the creative process was neither laborious nor slow. Simenon was a journeyman writer who churned out a book every few weeks.

Simenon's novels still remain on bookshelves today, particularly the 84 detective stories he wrote about the Parisian police detective, Inspector Maigret. Most of these stories take place in the streets of Paris, with the inspector occasionally venturing outside the capital to help his country cousins solve some puzzling crime. Maigret is a member of Paris's Police Judiciare, known as the PJ (pronounced pay-jay), and today the PJ's offices can be found on the quai des Orfèvres, not far from the official police headquarters at the Préfecture de Police, 1 rue de la Cité. Although Simenon set his stories about Inspector Maigret in Paris, the author himself did not stay in the city long. Simenon was an inveterate traveler, visiting dozens of countries and living for some time in both the United States and Switzerland, where he died in 1989.

JEAN RHYS

Another expatriate writer living in Paris was Jean Rhys. She was born on the West Indian island of Dominica in 1890, with a Welsh father and a Creole mother. She worked for a while as an actress in England before moving to Paris in 1920. There, the English author and editor Ford Madox Ford encouraged her to write. Ford edited the literary magazine called *Transatlantic Review*, which published works by authors such as Joyce, Hemingway, Stein, and Pound.

The stories Rhys wrote were set in the Left Bank world she inhabited, filled with artists, intellectuals, and bohemians. Her first book was a collection of these stories, called *The Left Bank*, which came out in 1927. The next year she published her first novel, *Postures*. The novel was later reissued under the title of *Quartet*, which was subsequently turned into a movie by director James Ivory. Ivory filmed some of the scenes in the café La Palette at 43 rue de Seine, which was and still remains a bohemian hangout that was frequented by Rhys.

After her early successes, Rhys later moved to England. There, she wrote nothing and lived anonymously, her books forgotten, until she produced her novel *Wide Sargasso Sea* in 1966. The novel, which imagines the life story of the madwoman in *Jane Eyre's* attic, regenerated her career and brought her earlier books back into print. Rhys died in England in 1979, having been a brief but bright flame in the Paris literary scene.

GEORGE ORWELL

Another brief visitor to the Parisian literary scene was the English author George Orwell. He produced a book that is an essential read about one facet of the city's subcultures that is not usually documented. Although many writers described the bohemian lifestyle of themselves and their friends, few of them knew very much about the world that Orwell describes in *Down and Out in Paris and London*. Published in 1933, this work was Orwell's first book. It provides a powerful and all-too-vivid look at the city's homeless poor, and the conditions in some of the hotel restaurants and kitchens where Orwell had worked as a lowly dishwasher.

Although the late 1920s and early 1930s that Orwell describes were periods of economic depression in many parts of the western world, France was less affected than most countries and life generally was reasonably secure for most people. That came to an end in 1932, when the world's Great Depression finally hit France. Equally troubling was the resurgence of power of Germany—one of France's oldest enemies—where the Fascists were taking control. The Second World War was looming. The good times would return eventually, but not until the Parisians had suffered through the nightmare of having their beloved City of Light occupied by a foreign power.

CHAPTER NINE

German Occupation and the New Wave

The young Americans who had flocked to Paris in the 1920s, excited by its freedom and cheap living, no longer felt so affluent or secure when fascist power rose in Germany during the late 1930s. The fear of Nazi power then was like the fear of terrorism today. As a result, many of the American authors, artists, and musicians living in Paris fled to the safety of America's shores. Some, such as Gertrude Stein, sought safety in the French countryside. Others, most notably Ernest Hemingway, would be back in Paris alongside the liberating army, ousting the German occupiers.

After the end of the First World War in 1918, a treaty had been signed in the Hall of Mirrors at Versailles in 1919 to deal with the German aggressors. Among the treaty's many conditions was a restriction on the size of the German armed forces and the establishment of demilitarized zones. By the late 1930s, under the dictatorial leadership of Adolf Hitler, many of these conditions were being breached.

In September 1939, Hitler's army invaded Poland. That action resulted in France and Britain declaring war on Germany. By 1940, the German army had invaded northern

France, and by 1942 southern France had also fallen to the advancing Nazi forces. In 1940, a French general named Charles de Gaulle began to organize a resistance army.

The United States had been supportive of France and Britain in their efforts to stop the German advances. By 1941, the Americans were themselves also at war against Germany. It was a long, devastating conflict but finally, on August 25, 1944, Paris was liberated and Allied troops were welcomed into the city as the Nazis fled. The following day, General de Gaulle entered Paris and organized a provisional government.

One member of the Allied troops who had liberated Paris was Ernest Hemingway. He was actually reporting for *Collier's* magazine but, ever keen to be near the action, Hemingway had talked himself into the ranks of the French troops who were first into the city. This made Hemingway one of the first Americans to enter the newly liberated Paris, just ahead of the U.S. Army itself. In an often-told tale, after liberating Paris Hemingway went to liberate the bar at the Ritz Hotel, where he had often gone to drink in the prewar days. The bar is now named the Hemingway Bar in his honor.

Hemingway's friend Sylvia Beach had closed her bookshop during the German occupation of Paris. Before the Germans arrived in the city she had managed to hide much of her stock. Beach herself was not as lucky, and she was later was arrested and sent to an internment camp. After a French friend intervened on her behalf, Beach was released.

AMERICAN AUTHORS RETURN TO PARIS

One member of the American troops that liberated Paris was a man named Irwin Shaw. Shaw was part of the team responsible for filming and recording the events, and so he registered at the headquarters of the foreign press corps in Paris, based at the Hôtel Scribe, 1 rue Scribe. Irwin Shaw later lived in an apartment at 24 rue du Boccador, where he worked on *The Young Lions*. This book is about the war in Europe, and features a character based on Ernest Hemingway. Hemingway was so annoyed at the obvious and unflattering portrait that he threatened to punch Shaw when the book came out. In addition to *The Young Lions*, Shaw went on to write screenplays and popular novels including *Two Weeks in Another Town* and *Rich Man, Poor Man*.

Irwin Shaw was not the only would-be author to stay at the Hôtel Scribe while in Paris. Another American writer who stayed there during the same time as Shaw was John Dos Passos. He went on to write *Manhattan Transfer* and the *U.S.A.* trilogy of novels. In addition to Dos Passos, Shaw's roommate at the Hôtel Scribe, William Saroyan, also went on to become an award-winning writer. Saroyan had been born to Armenian immigrants living in Fresno, California. As a young man, he became a private in the Signal Corps and then went on to make a name for himself in the literary world. In 1940, his play *The Time of Your Life* won the Pulitzer Prize. That year he also published a collection of short stories called *My Name Is Aram*, and in 1943 he wrote a novel called *The Human Comedy*.

Shaw's other Parisian home at 24 rue du Boccador also became a popular address for American writers. Humorist and journalist Art Buchwald lived there while writing postwar stories about Paris for the *Herald Tribune*. In addition, while living at 24 rue du Boccador, Theodore H. White wrote his war novel *The Mountain Road*, which went on to win the Pulitzer Prize. Also among Shaw's friends was the novelist James Salter, who describes their first meeting in Paris in his beautiful memoir *Burning the Days*:

> In my hand is a blue square of paper, the blue of Gauloises, and slowly I unfold it once more. I feel the excitement still. The creases have acquired a memory, opening, they reveal the invitation:
>
> *Can you meet me for a drink Relais bar Hotel Plaza Athénée Saturday evening seven P.M.?*

It is signed simply, *Shaw.*

November, the darkness coming on early, or perhaps December, late in the fall and the year, 1961. The city, as I thought of it, was like a splendid photograph, every wide avenue, every street. I had never met a writer of distinction. My agent, who was Irwin Shaw's agent also, had given him my name, and I was driving to Paris to meet him, coming in from the chill provinces by way of the thrilling diagonal that ran on the map from Chaumont, up through Troyes, to the very heart. (194)

That Salter misses the appointment turns out not to matter: "I went into the Relais. The first thing I saw was a solidly built man standing at the bar in an open trench coat, a copy of *Le Monde* stuffed in one pocket. I recognized him instantly. 'That's all right,' he said as I stumbled through an apology, 'what are you drinking?' It was quintessentially him" (195). To judge by Salter's account, in Paris, at the "very heart," everything seems to be quintessentially itself, even to achieve a sacred quality, though of the kind of sacredness that is diminished not at all by an admixture of the epicurean: "… there was more than a hint of another life, free of familiar inhibitions, a sacred life, this great museum and pleasure garden evolved for you alone" (198).

JEAN-PAUL SARTRE AND SIMONE DE BEAUVOIR

It seemed that within days of Paris's liberation, there were now just as many notable American writers in the city as there had been back in the 1920s. French writers were busy during those days, too. France's leading intellectual of those pre- and postwar days was Jean-Paul Sartre.

Sartre was born in Paris in 1905, and had been educated there as well as in Switzerland and in Germany. He was a teacher of philosophy first in Le Havre on the northern French coast, and later in Paris at the Lycée Henri IV at 23 rue Clovis in the Latin Quarter. Sartre's first novel, *La nausée* (*Nausea*), was published in 1938, and Sartre continued to write during the war years. Sartre did not escape the war unscathed, however. He had been a member of the French Resistance and had also been imprisoned by the Germans. After the war, in 1964, Sartre was awarded the Nobel Prize for Literature, although he declined it. Sartre's lifelong companion was the writer Simone de Beauvoir, who he had known since he was a student. De Beauvoir is best known for her nonfiction work *Le deuxième sexe* (*The Second Sex*), which came out in 1949 and was a precursor of the feminist movement in the way it analyzed women's roles in society.

Sartre and de Beauvoir are the two writers probably most associated with the Parisian Left Bank café society, and in particular with the Café de Flore at 172 boulevard St-Germain. Sartre described how they would sit in the café writing from 9 in the morning until noon, when they would go out for lunch, returning to the café to work for the rest of the day. For a long time, the couple lived just a few blocks away from the café in a room at the La Louisiane hotel, at 60 rue de Seine, just off the boulevard St-Germain.

Café de Flore was far from being the only unofficial office for Sartre and de Beauvoir. There were also periods when they set up a daily base at another café, Le Dôme, at the junction of boulevards Raspail and Montparnasse, where the two could be found from breakfast onward. Another favored haunt of Sartre and de Beauvoir was the Pavillon de Montsouris, a restaurant in the Parc Montsouris not far from Montparnasse to the south of the city center.

Sartre died in Paris in 1980. He had been raised to such heights in Parisian society that 50,000 people followed his hearse to the cemetery. After Sartre's death, de Beauvoir wrote a memoir, *Adieux*, of her time with Sartre in 1984. She died in Paris, in 1986. The couple is buried together in the cemetery of Montparnasse.

EXPATRIATE WRITERS IN PARIS
One of Jean-Paul Sartre's fellow existentialist philosopher-writers was Albert Camus. Camus had been born in Algeria in

1913, and came to Paris in 1940 to work on the newspaper, *Paris-Soir*. He immediately became an active member of the French Resistance Movement, and published his first novel, *L'Étranger* (*The Stranger*) in 1942. In 1947 came another well-received novel, *La peste* (*The Plague*), and Camus continued to live in Paris, writing plays, fiction, and nonfiction. He was also involved in the publishing of literary magazines. During the course of their relationship, Camus and Sartre often had arguments, and Camus's refusal to accept the Nobel Prize for Literature in 1957 may have been one reason why Sartre turned down the award just a few years later. In 1960, Camus was killed in a car crash near Sens, about 60 miles (97 km) southeast of Paris.

Another writer born overseas but later making his home in Paris was the absurdist dramatist Eugène Ionesco. Born in Romania in 1912, Ionesco had received some education in Paris and finally settled there in 1940, the same year as Camus. Ionesco was rather a different kind of writer, however. In his 1960 play *Rhinoceros*, the characters are slowly turning into rhinoceroses, demonstrating the consequences of conformity. In *Les chaises* (*The Chairs*) an elderly couple talks to nonexistent guests. In 1950, Ionesco wrote *La cantatrice chauve* (*The Bald Soprano*) and in 1951 *La leçon* (*The Lesson*). Ever since then, these two plays have been in performance at the Théâtre de la Huchette at 23 rue de la Huchette. It is a tiny, 85-seat theater in St-Germain. Ionesco was elected to the Académie française in 1970 and died in Paris in 1994.

Another proponent of the theater of the absurd, and following in the footsteps of those other notable Irish writers who had come to Paris earlier, was Samuel Beckett. Like fellow countryman James Joyce, Beckett was born in Dublin in 1906 and sought exile from his native Ireland as a young man. Beckett arrived in Paris in 1928 to teach, although he only finally settled in the city permanently in the late 1930s. There he met Joyce, and in fact Beckett's first published work had been an essay on James Joyce written in 1929. Later, with his own literary credentials established, he helped Joyce when he was struggling with the manuscript of his vast, complex work, *Finnegans Wake*.

When he arrived in Paris, Beckett taught at the École Normal Supérieure on rue d'Ulm. It was a prestigious job at a prestigious school, but not one that paid particularly well, and so during his first years in the city he had little money. In his early days, Beckett lived at the Hôtel Libéria, which is now the Best Western on rue de la Grande-Chaumière. He very quickly became a regular at the several cafés popular with writers and artists, such as La Closerie des Lilas at 171 boulevard du Montparnasse, La Coupole at 102 boulevard du Montparnasse, Le Dôme at 108 boulevard du Montparnasse, and Le Select 99 boulevard du Montparnasse. His favorite place to eat, however, was the Cochon de Lait, now renamed La Bastide-Odéon, at 7 rue de Corneille.

In 1942 Beckett left Paris, and the occupying Germans, to live for a time in southern France with his lifelong partner, Suzanne Deschevaux-Dumesnil. The two had met while Beckett was recovering in the hospital after being stabbed in a random attack on the street. The couple joined the French Resistance, returning to Paris after the Nazis were vanquished.

Beckett's home for many years was at 6 rue des Favorites, and he was another regular visitor to Shakespeare and Company at 12 rue de l'Odéon. There he had his one and only meeting with Ernest Hemingway, which was not a success since Hemingway was very critical of *Finnegans Wake*, the masterwork by Beckett's friend James Joyce.

Beckett's own masterwork was the play *Waiting for Godot*, which had its world premier in Paris in 1953 at the Théatre de Babylone. The theater, which stood on rue de Babylone, is no longer there today. Beckett wrote in French, and only later translated his works into what had been his native language, English. This furthers the notion that Beckett saw Paris as his home. Beckett's last work to be written in English was his novel *Watt*, published in 1953.

For a time, Beckett lived at 38 boulevard St-Jacques. He continued to live a quiet and slightly reclusive life in Paris and he received the Nobel Prize for Literature in 1969. In 1989, Beckett died in his Paris apartment on rue Rémy-Dumoncel, and the apartment has long since been demolished. Beckett is buried in a simple grave in the cemetery at Montparnasse.

AFRICAN AMERICAN WRITERS IN PARIS

In the 1920s and 1930s, the American artists living in Paris were predominantly either white writers or black musicians—the city had long been a home for jazz artists and singers. In the postwar years, there was an influx of African-American writers. It could be regarded as a trend, although in part it was due to the fact that more African-American writers were being published, so inevitably some of them would find themselves in Paris.

For African-American writers, though, the city did have a special attraction. There they could escape the prejudice of their own country. The South was still segregated, but even outside of the South many writers experienced prejudice. There was little of such prejudice in Paris, at least not against African Americans. Any prejudice that existed was generally directed against the many North African immigrants who came to France from its former colonies in places such as Algeria, Morocco, and Tunisia. Yet people of color from America and the Caribbean found themselves welcome.

The first major black writer to move to Paris was Richard Wright, known for the 1940 novel *Native Son* and the autobiographical *Black Boy*, which was published five years later. Wright had been born near Natchez, Mississippi, in 1908 and knew prejudice from the start. He had a succession of menial jobs as he traveled the South looking for work before he wound up in Chicago in 1935, where he began to write.

Wright achieved great literary success in the early 1940s, but in his native land he still faced prejudice. He moved to the more welcoming streets of Paris in the late 1940s, and from 1948 to 1959 he lived in a third-floor apartment at 14 rue Monsieur-le-Prince in St-Germain. This same street had once been the address of the poet Longfellow, who lived briefly at number 49, and the artist Whistler, whose studio was at number 22. A plaque on the wall marks Wright's residence and indicates the status he had in his newly adopted home. Wright had always fought for racial equality, and in 1959 civil rights leader Martin Luther King Jr. visited Wright in his apartment. Throughout his life, Wright traveled extensively and wrote about those travels. He also continued to delve into his own early life for material for his books. He died in Paris in 1960.

From the same generation as Wright came Chester Himes, who had been born in Missouri in 1909. In 1929, Himes began a seven-year jail term for armed robbery, and it was during his time in Ohio State Penitentiary that he began to write. Instead of committing crimes, he began to write about them and became one of the most highly regarded crime writers of the late 20th century. In 1953, he made the move to Paris, and it was while living there that he wrote his best work—not about Paris, but about Harlem.

Like other African-American authors, Himes mainly wanted to escape from the prejudice he found in the United States. He chose to move to Paris partially because his books were even more highly regarded in France than in his own country. Himes's novel *Lonely Crusade*, which dealt with racial issues in the labor movement had been poorly received in the United States. In 1952, however, it was chosen as one of the five best American books published in France, alongside writers of such stature as Hemingway, Fitzgerald, and William Faulkner.

Himes knew Richard Wright, and Wright met him on his arrival in Paris and tried to help him settle in to life in the city. After travels to southern France and to London, Himes eventually found a room at the Hôtel Jeanne d'Arc on rue de Buci, but discovered he had not totally left prejudice behind; the hotel's owners made it clear they did not approve of Himes's white girlfriend. Despite this episode, Himes continued to focus on his writing. In 1956, he came up with the two black detectives— Coffin Ed Johnson and Grave Digger Jones—who would be featured in several of his Harlem crime novels. At the time

Himes was penniless, but the creation of these two characters provided him with some financial security.

Himes's spent most of his time traveling, though when he returned to Paris he stayed in a rundown hotel at 8 rue Gît-le-Coeur, which is now the vastly more fashionable Relais Hôtel de Vieux Paris. Himes soon wrote about his experiences on the Left Bank in Paris, and those of other African-Americans, in his novel *A Case of Rape*. It was published in France in 1963 as *Une affair de viol*, but it was not translated into English until after his death. Two of the characters are loosely based on Richard Wright and James Baldwin, another African American writer living in Paris. In 1968, Himes moved to Spain where he died in 1984.

The third successful black American writer to live for a time in Paris was James Baldwin. There is a danger in linking Baldwin, Wright, and Himes together, however, because they did not always get along with each other. In particular, Baldwin was very envious of Wright's eminent position. Baldwin seemed to see it as his duty, as the younger writer, to become more successful than Wright.

Baldwin had been born in 1924 in the Harlem that Himes would recreate so vividly from the distance of his self-imposed European exile. In 1948, Baldwin moved to Paris with the aid of a fellowship, and lived there for the next eight years. The first place Baldwin visited in Paris, taken straight there from the airport by a friend, was Les Deux Magots, where he immediately met Richard Wright, and where he would later meet Chester Himes. For a time Baldwin took a room at the Hôtel Verneuil, 18 rue de Verneuil in St-Germain. The room had no heat in the winter, so Baldwin adopted the Paris tradition of working in cafés, in his case preferring the Café de Flore at 172 boulevard St-Germain. Later, Baldwin lived at the Grand Hôtel du Bac, on rue du Bac.

All the time Baldwin spent working at the cafés paid off, and it was in Paris that he completed his first novel, *Go Tell It on the Mountain*. The book was published in 1953 and brought Baldwin literary acclaim. His talent was confirmed with *Gio-*

vanni's Room, published in 1956 and set in the world of Paris's Left Bank, which Baldwin had gotten to know. By 1953, however, Baldwin was tiring of life in Paris, and he spent some time living near Chartres and later New York. He eventually divided

Bookshops

The modern visitor to Paris may well want to buy a book or two, either as a souvenir of the visit or to read more about the City of Light, whether fact or fiction. There are numerous large bookstores, of the type that can be found in any city in the world, but there are also some specialty shops that are worth seeking out, too.

There is no more atmospheric place to browse that among the *bouquinistes* (second-hand booksellers) on the Left Bank of the Seine, more or less opposite the Notre-Dame Cathedral. These little green stalls are a great tradition in the city and operate at the whim of the owners. There are usually some *bouquinistes* open most days of the week, though the busiest periods are naturally Saturday and Sunday, in particular Sunday mornings. The stalls sell books in all languages, although naturally the bulk of the stock is made up of French publications. In addition to books, the bouquinistes also sell magazines, comics, sheet music, posters, and postcards,

Close by the *bouquinistes* is the famous Shakespeare and Company bookshop, where there are many bargains to be had, as well as some high-priced rarities, too. Other shops in the city specialize in cookbooks, women's literature, and African books. Other stores specialize in comic books, an art form that is highly regarded in France, which is the home of famous comic-book characters such as Tintin and Asterix. Many of the museums—including the Louvre, the Pompidou Center, and the Musée d'Orsay—also have fine bookshops specializing in art.

his time between New York and his home in Saint-Paul in the south of France, where he died in 1987.

THE BEATNIKS

Another wave of American writers arrived in Paris in the 1950s: the Beatniks. So many of the major Beatnik writers visited Paris that the hotel where they invariably stayed, at 8 rue Gît-le-Coeur where Chester Himes lived, was nicknamed the Beat Hotel. Jack Kerouac, Allen Ginsberg, William S. Burroughs, Lawrence Ferlinghetti, and Gregory Corso all lived at this address at some time, either briefly or for longer periods. Burroughs and Ginsberg were both staying there when Ginsberg helped Burroughs prepare his novel *Naked Lunch* for its eventual publication in 1959.

None of the Beatniks ever settled permanently in Paris; they were all much too restless for that. Instead, there was a fluid movement between places such as New York, London, Paris, San Francisco, Mexico, and Morocco. Ferlinghetti did study in the city, however, and received a doctorate from the Sorbonne, the University of Paris, in 1951. Ginsberg lived there longer than most, and has described how he walked the Left Bank streets, aware of the ghosts of Rimbaud, Baudelaire, and Apollinaire. Upon visiting the cemetery of Père-Lachaise, he was inspired to write a poem called "At Apollinaire's Grave."

The Beatniks were the last great movement of American writers to gravitate toward Paris, although the city continues to attract writers, whether as a home or just as a subject matter. The most notable American writer to make Paris his base in more recent years is Edmund White. Born in Ohio in 1940, White had published several successful books before achieving greater celebrity with his gay novel, *A Boy's Own Story*, in 1982. The following year a Guggenheim Fellowship took him to Paris, and he has made it his main home ever since. White has written some fine nonfiction works about the city, in particular *Our Paris*, which was published in 1994, and *The Flâneur*, which was released in 2001.

Fine fiction also still emanates from Paris, a city that has always inspired work that is both literary and popular. It continues to do so in novels such as Georges Perec's *Life: A User's Manual*, which appeared in 1978 and has been said to do for Paris what James Joyce's *Ulysses* did for Dublin. Perec creates a world in miniature, in 99 chapters that all take place in an apartment block, somewhere in the city.

Patrick Süskind's worldwide bestseller *Perfume*, first published in 1985, tells the strange story of a man born in 18th-century Paris who has no personal smell of his own but a heightened sense of smell, which turns him into both a great perfumer and a murderer.

For centuries, then, Paris has produced an astonishing and varied list of some of the world's greatest authors: Rabelais, Molière, Voltaire, Stendhal, Balzac, Flaubert, Hugo, Zola, Dumas, Maupassant, Verlaine, Rimbaud, Proust, Feydeau, Colette, Cocteau, and Sartre. As if that list were not enough, other writers have gravitated toward the city and been inspired by it, including such towering 20th-century figures as Hemingway, Joyce, and Beckett. No doubt the world's writers will continue to come to Paris, drawn to the brilliant cultural glow of the City of Light.

PLACES OF **INTEREST**

This listing begins in the first arrondissement and rotates outward, clockwise.

Note: Most museums, châteaux, and other attractions are closed on public holidays, and many are closed on Mondays.

ARRONDISSEMENT 1

The geographical center of Paris contains some of the city's greatest treasures including the Louvre, Palais-Royal, Tuilleries Gardens, and Les Halles.

COMÉDIE-FRANÇAISE (FRENCH COMEDY THEATER)

2, rue de Richelieu • Tel: 44 58 15 15
www.comedie-francaise.fr/indexes/index.php

Officially established in 1680 by Louis XIV as the state theater of France, the Comédie Française has been based in its current location since 1799. Molière's company was the founding troupe of this theater and his plays, along with other classical and modern productions, can still be seen there. Theater tours are available on the third Sunday of the month.

THE CONCIERGERIE

1, quai de l'Horloge • Tel: 53 73 78 50

Located in the Ile-de-la-Cité, The Conciergerie was part of the royal palace from the 10th century to the 14th century. Much of the medieval construction dates to the rule of Philippe IV (1285–1314). When Charles V moved the royal palace to the Louvre, the Conciergerie became a prison, and during the Reign of

Terror, many of those sent to the guillotine were housed there. As Dickens writes in *A Tale of Two Cities*, "In the black prison of the Conciergerie, the doomed of the day awaited their fate." Among the prison's famed prisoners were Marie-Antoinette, Georges Danton, and Maximilien Robespierre. Open daily.

LE GRAND VÉFOUR

17, rue de Beaujolais • Tel: 42 96 56 27

This dining spot dating back to the reign of Louis XV remains a popular restaurant today. Authors Collette, Victor Hugo and Jean Cocteau were known to dine at this fine culinary establishment. Open Monday–Friday for lunch and dinner, closed in August.

HEMINGWAY BAR

Ritz Hotel • Entrance off rue Cambon • Tel: 43 16 33 65

Located in the Ritz Hotel, the Hemingway Bar is named after one of America's most famous literary expatriates, who spent much time there. F. Scott Fitzgerald, who also frequented the Ritz's hotel bar, used the hotel's name in his well-known short story, "The Diamond as Big as the Ritz." The Hemingway Bar is open daily, evenings only.

THE LOUVRE

Louvre Palace • 34, quai du Louvre • Tel: 40 20 53 17
www.louvre.fr

Begun as a fortification in 1190, the Louvre has undergone numerous transformations. Dating back to 1608 when Henri IV opened up the palace to artists, and the eventual inauguration of the Musée Central des Arts in 1793, the Louvre has been home to one of the richest art collections in the world. The former royal palace now houses Paris's principal collection of art, including celebrated exhibits such as the *Mona Lisa* and the *Venus de Milo*. Open Wednesday–Monday, closed Tuesday, late-night opening Wednesday and Monday.

PALAIS-ROYAL

Palais-Royal (Royal Palace) • place du Palais-Royal
www.palais-royal.org/

Originally built in 1636, the Palais-Royal became a hub of intellectualism as well as vice between the years 1784 and 1830. In his time, Diderot was known to frequent the cafés, but by the time Colette came to reside at 9 Rue de Beaujolais, the Palais had already assumed a more subdued and serene atmosphere. The Royal Palace's buildings are closed to the public, but its gardens and arcades are open daily.

ARRONDISSEMENT 2

Primarily a business district, both the Bourse (Paris stock market) and the Bibliothèque Nationale (Richelieu location) are located here.

BIBLIOTHÈQUE NATIONAL DE FRANCE
(NATIONAL LIBRARY-RICHELIEU LOCAION)

58, rue de Richelieu • Tel: 47 03 81 26
http://www.bnf.fr/

The National Library traces its origin back to King Charles V when it was founded at the Louvre in 1368. By 1537 it had become law that one copy of every book printed in France must be deposited in the library. Under the rule of Louis XIV the royal collections were moved to two houses on rue Vivienne which served as the basis for the rue de Richelieu location. The main collection was moved to the site François-Mitterand located in the 13th. Open daily.

HARRY'S NEW YORK BAR

5, rue Daunou • 75002 • Tel: 42 61 71 14

Dating back to 1911, this American cocktail bar claims to be the birthplace of the Bloody Mary and is recognized as the original

Harry's New York Bar. It quickly became a favorite among writers and is renowned for its ties to Hemingway. It is open daily.

ARRONDISSEMENT 4

The center of the Marais, one of the oldest neighborhoods in Paris, this section boasts the Pompidou Center, Notre-Dame Cathedral, and Place des Vosges.

MAISON DE VICTOR HUGO (VICTOR HUGO MUSEUM)

6, place des Vosges • Tel: 42 72 10 16

Between 1832 and 1848 the great French writer and thinker Victor Hugo lived on the second floor of the former Hôtel de Rohan-Guéménee in the Place des Vosges. His apartment, now a museum depicts various periods of the writer's life and contains a reconstruction of his death chamber with the bed in which he died. Open Tuesday–Sunday.

NOTRE-DAME CATHEDRAL

place du Parvis-Notre-Dame • Tel: 42 34 56 10
and 44 32 16 70

Described by Victor Hugo as "a vast symphony of stone," Notre-Dame ranks among the most famous cathedrals in the world. Begun in 12th century the gothic cathedral took nearly 180 years to complete, yet by the time of Napoléon's coronation, Notre-Dame was in such a state of severe disrepair that it was in jeopardy of being torn down. Thanks to Hugo's efforts, money was raised and the cathedral was restored. Among Notre-Dame's religious treasures are the Crown of Thorns, a Holy Nail, and a fragment of the True Cross, although these relics are only on display on Good Friday. Open daily.

PLACE DE LA BASTILLE

The Colonne de Juillet dominates this square and marks the site of the famous prison, the Bastille. July 14, Bastille Day, serves as the French national holiday to commemorate the storming and destruction of the infamous prison at the start of the French revolution in 1789. Among some of the famous writers imprisoned in the Bastille were the Marquis de Sade and Voltaire.

ARRONDISSEMENT 5

Also known as the Latin Quarter—a name derived from the fact that Latin was the common language at the Sorbonne during the middle ages—this neighborhood is home to the Sorbonne, the seat of learning in Paris. Other sights include the Panthéon and the Shakespeare and Company bookstore.

LYCÉE LOUIS LE GRAND

123 rue Saint Jacques
http://lyc-louis-le-grand.scola.ac-paris.fr/

Founded in 1563 and located very near the Sorbonne, the Lycée Louis le Grand is a state high school where the elites of France study. Some of the famous students from this elite school include Voltaire, Molière, and Victor Hugo.

MUSÉE DES COLLECTIONS HISTORIQUES DE LA PRÉFECTURE DE POLICE (POLICE MUSEUM)

1, bis rue des Carmes • Tel: 44 41 52 50

Located in the 5th district the Police Museum displays historical evidence and documents relating to the criminal aspects of the city. Among the historical uniforms and weapons are rare documents and testimonies including the statement Verlaine made about his crime of shooting the young poet Arthur Rimbaud. Open Monday through Saturday.

THE PANTHÉON

place du Panthéon • Tel: 44 32 18 00

Commissioned in 1754 by Louis VX to Jacques Germain Soufflot, the Panthéon was built as a church to Sainte-Geneviève. Completed in 1790, the same year the government abolished all monastic orders, the building was declared a "temple to the Nation," and authors Voltaire and Rousseau were buried there. Through much of the 19th century the Panthéon was used alternately as a church and a monument for the nation, until 1885 when it was made into a mortuary during the state funeral for Victor Hugo. The Panthéon serves as the resting place for Voltaire, Jean-Jacques Rousseau, Victor Hugo, Émile Zola, André Malraux, and Alexandre Dumas among others. Open daily.

RUE MOUFFETARD MARKET

Ernest Hemingway lived around the corner from this open-air market on one of Paris's oldest streets, and described the Place de la Contrescarpe at the north end of the street in *The Snows of Kilimanjaro*. Balzac also depicted it in *Père Goriot*. Rue Mouffetard Market is open Tuesday–Sunday, mornings only.

SHAKESPEARE AND COMPANY

37, rue de la Bûcherie • Tel: 43 26 96 50

Although this is not the original location, the spirit of Shakespeare and Company lives on at the new premises under the ownership of George Whitman. The shop functioned as an unofficial lending library to struggling writers and eventually began to publish books. It is open daily to visitors.

THÉÂTRE DE LA HUCHETTE

23, rue de la Huchette • Tel: 43 26 38 99

Dramatist Eugène Ionesco, who made his home in Paris, had two plays performed at this theater: *La cantatrice chauve* (*The Bald*

Soprano) and *La leçon* (*The Lesson*). The plays have been performed here since 1951. Open Monday–Saturday.

ARRONDISSEMENT 6

Separated from the 5th Arrondissement by Boulevard St. Michel, this section of the city contains a bit of the Latin Quarter, and is famous for its many cafés. It is also home to the site of the former Sylvia Beach bookstore, Shakespeare and Company (12 Rue de l'Odéon).

27 RUE DE FLEURES

Perhaps one of the most important literary salons in Paris was Gertrude Stein's collective at 27 rue de Fleures. Stein's brother Leo had first moved into the apartment at this location and was followed by Stein in 1904. Among the long list of artists who visited Stein were Ezra Pound, Sherwood Anderson (who then encouraged Hemingway to visit), and Pablo Picasso.

LA BASTIDE-ODÉON

7, rue de Corneille • Tel: 43 26 03 65

La Bastide was Samuel Beckett's favorite restaurant when it was formerly the Cochon de Lait. Despite the name change, it remains a world-class dining experience. Open Tuesday–Saturday.

BRASSERIE LIPP

151, boulevard St-Germain • Tel: 45 48 53 91

Founded in 1880 by Léonard Lipp, this brasserie has always been host to famous writers, politicians, and entertainers. It was a favorite haunt of André Gide and Oscar Wilde, and Marcel Proust routinely sent for beer from across town. Hemingway, who also frequented the brasserie describes a meal there in his work *A Moveable Feast*. The Brasserie is open daily.

CAFÉ DE FLORE

172, boulevard St-Germain • Tel: 45 48 55 26

Founded in 1865, this café on the Left Bank is a must visit for all tourists. The central figures of the Existentialist movement, Camus, Sartre, and de Beauvoir, met here. Open daily from 7am to 1:30am.

LA CLOSERIE DES LILAS

171, boulevard du Montparnasse • Tel: 40 51 34 50

One of Hemingway's favorite spots to sit and write, this famous watering hole has also been frequented by Jean-Paul Sartre and Samuel Beckett. It is open daily for lunch and dinner.

LES DEUX MAGOTS

6, place St-Germain-des-Prés • Tel: 45 48 55 25

Another of Paris's famous cafés located along the Left Bank, Les Deux Magots was founded in 1885, and is named after the two wooden statues that dominate the interior. Writer and activist Jean-Paul Sartre was a regular at this café as well as at the competing café next door, Café de Flore. Open daily.

JARDIN DU LUXEMBOURG (LUXEMBOURG GARDENS)

boulevard Saint-Michel • Tel: 42 34 20 00

Described as a green oasis in the heart of the city the Luxembourg Palace and Gardens were commissioned by Marie de Médici in the early 17th century and both were modeled after Florence's Pitti Palace and Boboli Gardens. The gardens encompass over 50 acres of open space and feature fountains and numerous attractions for children. There is a memorial to the great writer Stendhal and Hemingway claims to have fed off of the pigeons when he had fallen on hard times, later saying that the gardens "kept us from starvation…" in reference to "the classiness of its pigeons." Open daily.

LAPÉROUSE

51, quai des Grands-Augustins • Tel: 43 26 68 04

Founded in 1766 by a wine merchant, this restaurant was later frequented by Émile Zola, George Sand, Alexandre Dumas and Victor Hugo. Open Monday–Friday for lunch and dinner, Saturday for dinner.

LA PALETTE

43, rue de Seine • Tel: 43 26 68 15

Originally opened in 1903, La Palette was often frequented by author Henry Miller. Today it is one of Paris's hottest nightspots. Open Monday–Saturday, closed in August.

POLIDOR BISTRO

41, rue Monsieur-le-Prince • Tel: 43 26 95 34

Established in 1845 in the Latin Quarter near the Sorbonne, this popular bistro has played host to many intellectuals and students enjoying traditional French cuisine. It became a favorite restaurant of Hemingway's and other American expatriates. Open from noon to 12:30am Monday–Saturday for lunch and dinner, and noon to 11pm Sunday.

LE PROCOPE

13, rue de l'Ancienne-Comédie • Tel: 40 46 79 00
www.procope.com/anglais/default.htm

Considered to be the first literary café, Le Procope was opened in 1686 by Francesco Procopio dei Coltelli. Among its famed clientele were Voltaire, Rousseau, Balzac, and Victor Hugo. Le Procope is open daily for lunch and dinner.

LE SELECT

99, boulevard du Montparnasse • Tel: 45 48 38 24

This large, self-styled "American" bar was a favorite of Ernest Hemingway and Samuel Beckett. Open 7am–3am Monday–Thursday, and Sunday; 7am–4am Friday–Saturday.

ARRONDISSEMENT 7

Known for fine restaurants and perhaps the most easily recognized symbol of Paris, the Eiffel Tower, the 7th district is full of tourist attractions including the Musée d'Orsay and the École Militaire.

LES INVALIDES, EGLISE DU DÔME

place Vauban • Tel: 44 42 37 72

Commissioned in 1670 by Louis XIV, Les Invalides was France's first hospital and lodging facility dedicated solely for the care of the nation's veterans. The church, with its landmark dome, is the final resting place for Napoléon. Also entombed at Les Invalides is the French aviator and writer Antoine Marie-Roger de Saint-Exupery, author of *The Little Prince*. Open daily.

RODIN MUSEUM

77, rue de Varenne • Tel: 44 18 61 10
www.musee-rodin.fr/

Formerly a collection of artists' studios at the Hôtel de Biron, the house was converted to the Rodin Museum after August Rodin had lived in and assembled his work there. The Parisian author Jean Cocteau had lived at the Hôtel for a time before it became the world-renowned museum in 1919. It is open Tuesday through Sunday.

TOUR EIFFEL

Champ de Mars • Tel: 44 11 23 23
http://www.tour-eiffel.fr/teiffel/uk/

Guy de Maupassant, a staunch opponent of the tower, once commented after visiting the landmark, "it is the only place, from which I don't see it." Indeed the city's most recognizable landmark had many critics, and in 1887 they published the "Protest against the Tower of Monsieur Eiffel" in the newspaper *Le Temps*. Maupassant, Zola, and Cahrles Garnier were just a few of the 300 artists to sign the petition protesting the monument. Open daily.

ARRONDISSEMENT 8

While the 1st is the geographical center of the city, many consider the Arc de Triomphe in the 8th to be the symbolic center of France. Other attractions in the 8th include the Grand and Petit Palais, the Place de la Concorde, and La Madeleine.

ARC DE TRIOMPHE AND CHAMPS-ÉLYSÉES

place Charles-de-Gaulle • Tel: 55 37 73 77

Commissioned in 1806 by Napoléon as a monument to French military might and pride, the Arc de Triomphe stands 164 feet (50 m) high and 147 feet (45 m) wide, the largest arch of its kind. In 1840, Napoléon's ashes passed under the arch, and on May 22, 1885, Victor Hugo's body lay in state under the arch before being interred at the Panthéon. Also at the Arc lies the Tomb of the Unknown Soldier. Of the main avenues radiating from the Arc none is more famous than the Champs-Élysées. Once an elegant promenade lined with gas lamps, formal gardens, fountains and cafés, the Champs-Élysées is now crowded by fast-food stores and car dealerships. However, a walk along the famed avenue and through the *Jardin des Champs-Élysées* may still recall Proust and his protagonist's first love Gilbert. The Arc de Triomphe is open daily for access to both the top and the museum.

LE BOEUF SUR LE TOIT

34, rue du Colisée • Tel: 53.93.65.55

Once a meeting place for author Jean Cocteau and other surrealists, it was one of the centers for jazz in Paris in the 1930s. Le Boeuf is now an Art Deco brasserie. It is open seven days a week.

ARRONDISSEMENT 9

A mix of neighborhoods and grand boulevards, the 9th is home to the famous Café de la Paix and the grand opera house Opéra Garnier.

CAFÉ DE LA PAIX

3, place de l'Opéra • Tel: 40 07 30 20

Situated in the Grand Hotel the Café de la Paix is perhaps the most famous Parisian café. Built by Charles Garnier the Café retains much of its 19th century charm. Not only has the Café appeared in numerous literary works, but has been frequented by such literary luminaries as Émile Zola, Guy de Maupassant, Oscar Wilde, and Ernest Hemingway. Open daily for lunch and dinner.

MUSÉE DE LA VIE ROMANTIQUE (MUSEUM OF ROMANTIC LIFE)

16, rue Chaptal • Tel: 48 74 95 38

Originally belonging to painter Ary Scheffer and his nephew, the writer Ernest Renan, this house was converted into a museum of their lives and those of their circle of friends which included Chopin, Delacroix, and George Sand. The museum is intended to place the visitor into the artistic and literary life of the French Romantics. Open Tuesday–Sunday.

ARRONDISSEMENT 14

Best known for its cafés, and the 1920s bohemian Paris of Montparnasse, the 14th was frequented by Sartre, Hemingway and Picasso.

CIMETIÈRE MONTPARNASSE

3 Boulevard Edgar-Quinet • Tel: 40 71 75 60

Officially dedicated as a municipal cemetery in 1824, Montparnasse is the smallest of the three major Parisian cemeteries. Many of the world's great authors and intellectuals are buried in this cemetery, including Baudelaire, Guy de Maupassant, Jean-Paul Sartre, Simone de Beauvoir, and Samuel Beckett. Open daily.

LA COUPOLE

102, boulevard du Montparnasse • Tel: 43 20 14 20

With over 400 seats, this brasserie is one of the largest in Paris. Samuel Beckett became a regular at this brasserie when he arrived in Paris, and quickly fit in with the likes of Ernest Hemingway and Pablo Picasso. It is open daily.

LE DÔME

108, boulevard du Montparnasse • Tel: 43 35 25 81

Now home to an exclusive restaurant, Le Dôme was a café that used to be frequented by Jean-Paul Sartre and Simone de Beauvoir. Open daily, closed Sunday–Monday in August.

PAVILLON DE MONTSOURIS

Parc Montsouris • 20, rue Gazan • Tel: 45 88 38 52

This restaurant in the Parc Montsouris not far from Montparnasse was another haunt of Jean-Paul Sartre and Simone de Beauvoir. Open daily, lunch and dinner

ARRONDISSEMENT 15

Primarily residential, the 15th is the largest district in the city. In addition to the Tour Montparnasse, one can find book dealers on the weekends in the Parc George-Brassens, or view one of the oldest artists' colonies, La Ruche.

LA RUCHE

2, passage Dantzig

La Ruche literally means the beehive and is named so for its polygonal shape. It was created for the Universal Exhibition in 1900 by Gustav Eiffel, and rebuilt by French sculptor Alfred Boucher in 1902. The building became a workshop for artists and writers alike. It is believed that Marc Chagall painted over 30 works at La Ruche, and that writers Appolinaire and Max Jacob spent time there as did political figures Vladimir Lenin and Leon Trotsky. Because La Ruche is still an active artists' colony, studio visits are only available by permission of their occupants.

ARRONDISSEMENT 16

Quietly located on the outskirts of the city, the 16th is full of wealthy neighborhoods, small museums and Art Nouveau architecture.

MAISON DE BALZAC (BALZAC MUSEUM)

47, rue Raynouard • Tel: 55 74 41 80

Located on the outskirts of the city in arrondissement 16 is the Balzac Museum. This museum was once the home of Balzac where he lived under the pseudonym Monsieur de Breugnol. The museum contains a number of Balzac's personal affects including his writing desk where he undoubtedly worked on his masterpiece *La Comédie humaine* (*The Human Comedy*). Open Tuesday–Sunday.

ARRONDISSEMENT 18

In a word, Montmartre. In this unique village-like section one can find the famous cabaret Moulin Rouge as well as the Basilica of Sacré-Couer.

CIMETIÈRE MONTMARTRE

20, avenue Rachel • Tel: 43 87 64 24

Created in 1798, closed down, and then reopened in 1831, the cemetery at Montmartre serves as the final resting place for some of France's greatest literary and artistic figures. Stendhal, Alexandre Dumas, and Edgar Degas are all buried here. Émile Zola was interred here as well until his remains were moved to the Panthéon in 1908. The cemetery is accessible by stairs from rue Caulaincourt. Open daily from 8am to 6pm and Saturday from 8:30am to 6pm.

ARRONDISSEMENT 20

Primarily considered an outlying residential area, the 20th is home to the most visited cemetery in Paris, Père-Lachaise.

PÈRE-LACHAISE

Boulevard de Ménilmontant • Tel: 43 70 70 33

The largest cemetery in Paris Père-Lachaise opened in 1804, but was at first considered too remote to many Parisians. In an effort to attract status-conscious Parisians, the government transferred the remains of several famous people including Molière, Jean de La Fontaine, and the famed lovers Héloïse and Abélard. It is the final resting place for some of the most notable literary figures in Western History, including Honoré de Balzac, Molière, Marcel Proust, Oscar Wilde, Gertrude Stein and Richard Wright. Jim Morrison is also buried here, which attracts many of his fans and tourists. Entrances on rue des Rondeaux bd. de Menilmontant and

Rue de la Reunion. Open Easter–September, daily 8–6; October–Easter, 8am–dusk.

OUTSIDE THE CITY

VERSAILLES

www.chateauversailles.fr/

Built as a hunting lodge in 1623 by Louis XIII, Versailles was transformed by the Sun King, Louis XIV from a modest lodge to the epitome of opulence. The palace's association with the French aristocracy is inescapable, and it has been an integral and symbolic part of French history ever since Louis XIV moved his court there in 1682. While not a part of the city proper the Palace at Versailles is easily reached from central Paris on the RER train, line C, to the Versailles-Rive Gauche Station. It can get quite busy, especially on weekends and in the summer, so try to arrive early in the day to avoid waiting. Open Tuesday–Sunday.

300 B.C.	The Parisii settle on what is now the Île de la Cité.
52 B.C.	The Romans conquer the Parisii.
A.D. 508	Paris is made the capital of a new Frankish kingdom, established by Clovis.
725	Muslims attack Gaul.
768–814	Rule of Charlemagne.
1079	Birth of Pierre Abélard.
1163	Work starts on the present Notre-Dame Cathedral.
1167	Les Halles is created on the Right Bank.
1215	Paris University is founded, making it the only university in northern France.
1253	The Sorbonne is founded.
1370	Building of the Bastille commences.
1430	Henry VI of England is crowned king of France at Notre-Dame.
1453	The Hundred Years War against England comes to an end.
1469	The first French printing works starts at the Sorbonne.
1494	François Rabelais is born.
1546	Work starts on Louvre Palace.
1555	Poet and critic François de Malherbe is born.
1572	Protestants are massacred on St. Bartholomew's Day.
1610	Louis XIII ascends the throne marking the beginning of le grand siècle.
1612	Inauguration of Place des Vosges.

1621   Jean de la Fontaine is born.

1622   Jean-Baptiste Poquelin (Molière) is born.

1624   The Tuileries Palace are completed.

1626   Madame de Sévigné is born.

1629   The Palais-Royal is built.

1631   Paris's first newspaper, *La Gazette*, begins.

1634   Novelist Marie-Madeleine de la Fayette is born.

1639   Jean Baptiste Racine is born.

1643   King Louis XIII dies; Marie de Médici and Cardinal Mazarin assume control of the Regency.

1661   Accession of Louis XIV.

1667   The Louvre is rebuilt.

1670   The Hotel des Invalides is built.

1672   Paris's first daily newspaper, *Le journal de la ville de Paris*, begins.

1678   First important French novel, *Princess of Cleves*, is written by de la Fayette.

1682   The royal court moves from Paris to Versailles and will stay there until the Revolution.

1686   Paris's first café, Le Procope, opens.

1688   Playwright Pierre Carlet de Chamblain de Marivaux is born.

1689   Charles-Louis de Secondat (Baron de Montesquieu) is born.

1694   Voltaire (François Marie Arouet) is born.

1697   Novelist and cleric Abbé Prévost is born.

1702   Paris is divided into arrondissements.

1712   Jean-Jacques Rousseau is born.

1713   Denis Diderot is born.

1715   King Louis XIV dies.

1717	Mathematician and encyclopedist Jean Le Rond d'Alembert is born.
1722	The first fire brigade in Paris is founded.
1732	Dramatist Pierre-Augustin Caron de Beaumarchais is born.
1740	Marquis de Sade is born.
1741	Pierre Choderlos de Laclos is born.
1751	The first volume of Diderot's encyclopedia is published.
1750s	The Place de la Concorde is built.
1757	First streetlamps appear in Paris.
1762	Rousseau's *Emile and the Social Contract* are published.
1774	Louis XV dies; Louis XVI ascends the throne.
1778	France supports America in its fight for independence.
1782	The first sidewalks built.
1783	First ascent in a hot-air balloon is made by the Montgolfier Brothers; Marie-Henri Beyle (Stendhal) is born.
1789	The French Revolution begins, Parisians storm the Bastille, and the Declaration of the Rights of Man and the Citizen is adopted.
1791	Parisians storm the Tuileries Palace.
1792	King Louis XVI is overthrown, the monarchy is abolished, and France is declared a Republic.
1793	Louis XVI and Marie-Antoinette are executed.
1799	Napoléon takes power and heads the post-revolutionary government; Honoré de Balzac is born.
1802	Victor Hugo is born; Alexandre Dumas *père* is born.
1804	Napoléon is crowned emperor; Eugène Sue is born; George Sand is born.

1806	Building of the Arc de Triomphe begins.
1808	Poet and translator Gérard de Nerval is born.
1812	Napoléon is defeated in Russia.
1814	Napoléon abdicates.
1815	The Battle of Waterloo takes place; the monarchy is restored under Louis XVIII.
1821	Charles Baudelaire is born; Gustav Flaubert is born.
1824	Alexandre Dumas *fils* is born. Charles X succeeds to throne.
1830	Another revolution begins, this time bringing in the constitutional monarchy.
1831	*Notre Dame de Paris* (*The Hunchback of Notre Dame*) by Victor Hugo is published.
1840	Émile Zola is born.
1842	Stéphane Mallarmé is born.
1843	Henry James is born in America.
1844	Anatole France is born; Paul Verlaine is born.
1848	Monarchy in the form of Louis-Philippe is removed again.
1850	Guy de Maupassant is born.
1851	Napoléon III establishes the Second Empire.
1852–1870	Baron Georges Haussmann modernizes large parts of Paris.
1854	Arthur Rimbaud is born; Oscar Wilde is born in Ireland.
1857	Baudelaire is prosecuted for obscenity for the publication of *Les fleurs du mal* (*The Flowers of Evil*).
1862	*Les misérables* by Victor Hugo is published; playwright Georges Feydeau is born; Edith Wharton is born in America.
1868	Censorship of the press is eased.

1869   André Gide is born.

1870   The Siege of Paris occurs, Napoléon flees.

1871   Uprising of the Paris Commune begins; the Third
        Republic is established; Marcel Proust is born.

1873   Sidonie Gabrielle Colette is born; Ford Madox Ford
        born in England.

1874   Birth of impressionism with Manet's Impression:
        Soleil levant (Impression: The Sun Rising); Gertrude
        Stein is born in America.

1880   The poet Guillaume Apollinaire is born.

1882   James Joyce is born in Ireland.

1885   Ezra Pound is born in America.

1889   The Eiffel Tower is built; Jean Cocteau born.

1890   Jean Rhys is born in Dominica.

1891   Work begins on first métro (subway); Henry Miller is
        born in America.

1894   The Dreyfus Affair occurs; Louis-Ferdinand Céline
        is born.

1895   The Lumière brothers discover cinematography.

1896   F. Scott Fitzgerald is born in America.

1899   Ernest Hemingway is born in America. Universal
        Exposition is held.

1900   Universal Exposition is held and several permanent
        monuments are dedicated to it (Grand Palais, Petit
        Palais, Pont Alexandre III).

1901   André Malraux is born.

1903   Georges Simenon is born in Belgium; George Orwell
        is born in India.

1905   Jean-Paul Sartre is born.

1906   Samuel Beckett is born in Ireland.

1907   Picasso completes *Les Demoiselles d'Avignon.*

1908	Simone de Beauvoir is born; Richard Wright is born in America.
1909	Chester Himes is born in America.
1912	Eugène Ionesco is born in Romania.
1913	First volume of Marcel Proust's *À la recherche du temps perdu* (*Remembrance of Things Past*) is published; Albert Camus is born in Algeria.
1914–1918	World War I occurs.
1914	William Burroughs is born in America.
1919	Treaty of Versailles is signed.
1924	James Baldwin is born in America; André Breton publishes the *Surrealist Manifesto*.
1926	Allen Ginsberg is born in America.
1930s	Economic depression occurs, but the arts—especially literature—thrive.
1936	Georges Perec is born.
1937	The Palais de Chaillot is constructed.
1939–1945	World War II occurs, Paris is occupied by Nazi Germany from 1940 to 1944.
1940	Edmund White is born in America.
1949	Patrick Süskind is born.
1968	Student riots break out.
2002	France adopts the Euro as its currency.

BIBLIOGRAPHY

Baldwin, James. *Giovanni's Room*. New York: Dial Press, 1956.

Balzac, Honoré de. *La Comédie Humaine* (*The Human Comedy*). English version. Philadelphia: Gebbie Pub. Co., 1898–1900.

Baudelaire, Charles. *Flowers of Evil: A Selection*, eds. Marthiel and Jackson Matthews. New York: New Directions, 1955.

Beauvoir, Simone de. *Adieux: a farewell to Sartre*. Trans. Patrick O'Brian. New York: Pantheon Books, 1984.

Beyle, Marie-Henri (Stendhal). *The Red and the Black*, trans. C.K. Scott Moncrieff. New York: Modern Library, 1926.

Bishop, Morris, ed. *Eight Plays by Molière*, trans. Bishop. New York: Modern Library, 1957.

Blackmore, Ruth, et al. *Rough Guide to Paris*. New York, NY and London, UK: Rough Guides, 2003.

Carpenter, Humphrey. *Geniuses Together: American writers in Paris in the 1920s*. Boston: Houghton Mifflin Co., 1988.

Cocteau, Jean. *Les Enfants Terribles*. English Version. New York: New Directions, 1957.

Cole, Robert. *A Traveller's History of Paris*. New York: Interlink Books, 1994.

Culbertson, Judi & Randall, Tom. *Permanent Parisians: An Illustrated Guide to the Cemeteries of Paris*. London: Robson, 1991.

Dickens, Charles. *A Tale of Two Cities* (1859). New York: Alfred. A. Knopf, 1993.

Dumas, Alexandre (*père*). *Les Trois Mousquetaires* (*The Three Musketeers*, 1844), edited by David Coward. London: Oxford University Press, 1991.

Dunlop, F. and E. Morris. *Explorer Paris.* Basingstoke, UK: AA Publishing, 1999.

Fallon, Steve. *Lonely Planet Paris.* Oakland, CA and London, UK: Lonely Planet, 2002.

Flaubert, Gustave. *Madame Bovary* (1857), New York: Alfred A. Knopf, 1993.

Gide, André. Les Faux-Monnayeurs (*The Counterfeiters*, 1925), trans. by Dorothy Bussy. New York: Modern Library, 1955.

Hemingway, Ernest. *A Moveable Feast.* New York: Touchstone, 1992.

Hugo, Victor. *Notre-Dame de Paris* (The *Hunchback of Notre-Dame*, 1831), trans. by Alban Krailsheimer. Oxford; New York: Oxford University Press.

———. *Les Misérables* (1862), trans. by Charles E. Wilbour. New York: Modern Library, 1992.

James, Henry. *The Ambassadors* (1903), ed. by Christopher Butler. Oxford; New York: Oxford University Press, 1985.

———. *The American* (1877), ed. by Wiliam Spengemann. New York: Penguin Books, 1981.

Laclos, Choderlos de. *Dangerous Liaisons (Les Liaisons Dangéreuses),* trans. Richard Aldington. New York: Dutton, 1924.

Lottman, Herbert. *The Left Bank: writers, artists, and politics from the popular front to the Cold War.* Boston: Houghton Mifflin, 1982.

Malraux, André. *La Condition Humaine* (*The Human Condition,* 1933), trans. by Haakon M. Chevalier. New York: The Modern Library, 1936.

Miller, Henry. *Tropic of Cancer* (1934), New York: Grove Press, 1961.

———, *Tropic of Capricorn* (1939), New York: Grove Press, 1962.

Molière. *The Miser and Other Plays.* New York: Penguin, 1962.

Orwell, George. *Down and Out in Paris and London* (1933). New York: Harcourt Brace Jovanovich, 1961.

Perec, Georges. *La vie mode d'emploi* (*Life: A User's Manual,* 1978). trans. by David Bellos. Boston: D.R. Godine, 1987.

Proust, Marcel. *À La Recherche du Temps Perdu* (*Remembrance of Things Past*, 1913-27), trans. by C.K. Scott Montcrieff and Terence. New York: Random House, 1981.

————. *In Search of Lost Time, III: The Guermantes Way*, trans. C.K. Scott Moncrieff, Terence Kilmartin, and D.J. Enright. New York: Random House, 1993.

Racine, Jean-Baptiste. *Phèdre* (1677), trans. by Richard Wilbur. San Diego: Harcourt Brace Jovanovich, 1986.

Rousseau, Jean-Jacques. *The Confessions of Jean-Jacques Rousseau,* trans. J.M. Cohen. Harmondsworth: Penguin, 1953.

Rhys, Jean. *The Left Bank.* Preface by Ford Madox Ford. London: J. Cape, 1927.

Salter, James. *Burning the Days.* New York: Random House, 1997.

Sawyer-Lauçanno, Christopher. *The Continual Pilgrimage.* New York: Grove Press, 1992.

Stein, Gertrude. *The Autobiography of Alice B. Toklas.* New York: Harcourt Brace and Company, 1933.

Stendhal. *Le Rouge et le Noir* (*The Red and the Black*, 1830), trans. by Catherine Slater. Oxford; New York: Oxford University Press, 1991.

Süskind, Patrick. *Perfume* (Das Parfum, 1985), New York: Alfred A. Knopf, 1986.

Tillier, Alan. *Eyewitness Paris.* London, UK: Dorling Kindersley, 2003.

Time Out Paris. New York: Penguin Books, 2004.

Voltaire. *Candide* (1759), New York: W.W. Norton, 1991.

Warne, Sophie. *Footprint Paris.* Bath, UK: Footprint Handbooks, 2003.

Wilson, Arthur M. *Diderot.* New York: Oxford University Press, 1972.

White, Andrew, ed. *Time Out Book of Paris Walks.* New York: Penguin, 2000.

White, Edmund. *The Flâneur: a Stroll through the Paradoxes of Paris.* New York: Bloomsbury, 2001.

———. *Our Paris: sketches from memory.* New York: Alfred A. Knopf, 1994.

Wurman, Richard Saul. *Access Paris.* New York: HarperCollins, 2002.

Zola, Emile. *Les Rougon-Macquart series.* Paris: Fasquelle, 1967.

FURTHER READING

Campbell, James. *Exiled in Paris: Richard Wright, James Baldwin, Samuel Beckett and others on the Left Bank.* New York: Scribner, 1995.

Carpenter, Humphrey. *Geniuses Together: American writers in Paris in the 1920s.* Boston: Houghton Mifflin Co., 1988.

Cole, Robert. *A Traveller's History of Paris.* New York: Interlink Books, 1994.

Culbertson, Judi & Randall, Tom. *Permanent Parisians: An Illustrated Guide to the Cemeteries of Paris.* London: Robson, 1991.

Fitch, Noel R. *Walks In Hemingway's Paris: A Guide To Paris For The Literary Traveler.* New York: St. Martin's Press, 1992.

Gopnik, Adam, ed. *Americans in Paris.* New York: Library of America, 2004.

Gopnik, Adam. *Paris to the Moon.* New York: Random House, 2000.

Hemingway, Ernest. *A Moveable Feast.* New York: Touchstone, 1992.

Horne, Alistair. *Seven ages of Paris.* New York: Knopf, 2002.

Lee, Jennifer. *Paris in Mind.* New York: Vintage, 2003.

Lottman, Herbert. *The Left Bank: writers, artists, and politics from the popular front to the Cold War.* Boston: Houghton Mifflin, 1982.

Orwell, George. *Down and Out in Paris and London* (1933). New York: Harcourt Brace Jovanovich, 1961.

Rhys, Jean. *The Left Bank.* Preface by Ford Madox Ford. London: J. Cape, 1927.

White, Edmund. *The Flâneur: a Stroll through the Paradoxes of Paris.* New York: Bloomsbury, 2001.

———. *Our Paris: Sketches from Memory.* New York: Alfred A. Knopf, 1994.

WEBSITES

Discover France
www.discoverfrance.net/

The Paris Pages
www.paris.org

Paris – Wikipedia
en.wikipedia.org/wiki/Paris

United States Embassy in France
www.amb-usa.fr/

Webmuseum: Paris
www.ibiblio.org/wm/paris/

INDEX

Garnier, Charles, 120–21
Gaul, 8
    attack on, 126
Gaulle, Charles de, 92, 98
Gauthier-Villars, Henri, 80
Gazette, La, 127
Germinal (Zola), xv, 71
Gide, André, 67, 68, 116
    birth, 79, 130
    death, 79
Gigi (Colette), 80
Ginsberg, Allen, 108
    birth, 131
Giovanni's Room (Baldwin), 106–7
Girl from Maxim's, The. See Dame de chez Maxim, La (Feydeau)
Goethe, vii, x, xiv
Golden Poems, The. See Poèmes dorés, Les (France)
Good Friend. See Bel-Ami (Maupassant)
Go Tell It On the Mountain (Baldwin), 106
Goutte-d'Or, La (The Drop of Gold) district, 71
Grande Arche at La Défense, 5
Grande Café Capucines, 78
Grand Palais, 120, 130
Grand siècle, le, 10, 19–20, 126
Grand Véfour, Le, 80, 111
Gravity's Rainbow (Pynchon), xi
Great Depression, 96
Great Gatsby, The (Fitzgerald), xi
Guermantes Way, The (Proust), 81–82
Gulliver's Travels (Swift), 23

Halles, Les, 21, 51, 110
    creation, 8, 126
Hall of Mirrors, 11, 19, 97
Hanska, Éveline, 47–49
Harry's New York Bar, 88
Harvest of Helenism, The (Peters), viii
Haussmann, Georges–Eugène, 58, 129, A

Hawthorne, Nathaniel, x–xi
Heine, Heinrich, viii
Hemingway Bar, 111–13
Hemingway, Ernest, xi, 7, 93, 95, 105, H
    birth, 130
    Nobel prize, 84
    in Paris, x, 75, 83, 85–90, 103, 109, 111, 113, 115–19, 121–22
    and war, 97–98
Henriade, La (Voltaire), 24
Henry IV, King of France 53, 111
Henry VI, King of France, 10, 24, 126
Himes, Chester, 108
    birth, 105, 130
    death, 106
    imprisonment, 105
Histoire de ma vie (Sand), 55
History of Painting in Italy and Rome, Naples, and Florence (Stendhal), 42
Hitler, Adolf, 97
Homer, viii–ix
Horribles et èpouvantables faits et prouesses du très renommé Pantagruel, roy des Dipsodes, Les (Rabelais), 9
Hugo, Victor, x–xi, xiii, 3, 7, 22, 41, 54, 75, 129, F
    birth, 49, 128
    death, 51
    exile, xv, 51
    grave, 25, 51, 115
    home, 53
    museum, 3, 50
    in Paris, 91, 109, 111, 113–14, 118, 120
    and romanticism, xiv, 74
Human Comedy, The. See Comédie humanie, La (Balzac)
Human Comedy, The (Saroyan), 99
Human Condition, The. See Condition humaine, La (Malraux)

PICTURE **CREDITS**

CONTRIBUTORS

HAROLD BLOOM is Sterling Professor of the Humanities at Yale University. He is the author of over 20 books, including *Shelley's Mythmaking* (1959), *The Visionary Company* (1961), *Blake's Apocalypse* (1963), *Yeats* (1970), *A Map of Misreading* (1975), *Kabbalah and Criticism* (1975), *Agon: Toward a Theory of Revisionism* (1982), *The American Religion* (1992), *The Western Canon* (1994), and *Omens of Millennium: The Gnosis of Angels, Dreams, and Resurrection* (1996). *The Anxiety of Influence* (1973) sets forth Professor Bloom's provocative theory of the literary relationships between the great writers and their predecessors. His most recent books include *Shakespeare: The Invention of the Human* (1998), a 1998 National Book Award finalist, *How to Read and Why* (2000), *Genius: A Mosaic of One Hundred Exemplary Creative Minds* (2002), and *Hamlet: Poem Unlimited* (2003). In 1999, Professor Bloom received the prestigious American Academy of Arts and Letters Gold Medal for Criticism, and in 2002 he received the Catalonia International Prize.

MIKE GERRARD is a travel writer who has written or contributed to over 20 guidebooks along with three radio plays for the BBC. His awards include one from the British Guild of Travel Writers, and two from the Outdoor Writers' Guild. His travel books include the *National Geographic Traveler Guide to Greece* and Dorling Kindersley's *Top Ten Paris guide*.